P9-DNL-373

O T H E R   B O O K S *
by
Linda and/or Richard Eyre

3 Steps to a Strong Family
Teaching Your Children Values
Teaching Your Children Responsibility
Teaching Your Children Joy
A Joyful Mother of Children
The Awakening (a novel)
Children's Stories About Joy (volumes I and II)

If you have difficulty finding any of the above titles in book-stores, call (801) 581-0112 to order direct.

Richard Eyre

A FIRESIDE BOOK
Published by Simon & Schuster
NewYork London Toronto Sydney Tokyo Singapore

Don't Just Do Something, Sit There

New MAXIMS to
Refresh and Enrich Your Life

FIRESIDE
Rockefeller Center
1230 Avenue of the Americas
New York, New York   10020

FIRESIDE and colophon are registered trademarks
of Simon & Schuster Inc.

Designed by Crowded House Design

Manufactured in the United States of America

1   3   5   7   9   10   8   6   4   2

Library of Congress Cataloging-in-Publication Data is
available.

ISBN: 0-671-88729-7

Stress!
Hurry and worry.
Aggravation and frustration.
The world does it to us, doesn't it?
Fast pace, big demands, high expectations,
congestion and competition.
No.
We do it to ourselves. We do it in our minds.
We let the world in and *we put the pressure on ourselves*.
How you feel and how you live does not depend
on what goes on around you.
It depends on what goes on inside you — particularly inside
   your head.
The world is a hard place to change
and this book doesn't suggest that you change any of it.
This is a book about changing your mind,
about casting out some old, stress-producing attitudes or
   cliches
and replacing them with some softer, more mellow *maxims*.
This is not a how-to book, it is a how-to-think book.
The old cliches that it throws out
are more than quaint old sayings.
They are symbols of old thinking or wrong thinking
that *detract* from the joy of life.
The new maxims proposed are symbols of new attitudes
that are *designed* to enhance joy.

Richard Eyre
Washington, D.C.
1994

FOR MY ONCE AND FUTURE FRIEND

RICHARD ROSINE

Some of the catchy little sayings, proverbs,
or little notions of traditional wisdom
that people (and society) have been repeating to us
  over the years
don't work anymore.
In fact they aren't true anymore.
In fact they've become part of the problem,
rather than part of any solution.
And they're not just cute little cliches
or harmless, old-fashioned platitudes.
No!
They have worked their way into our subconscious
and influenced our attitudes.
They often prompt unrealistic expectations,
turn us into dissatisfied perfectionists,
or give us inaccurate perceptions
  of the world around us.

They also produce stress.

Some of these old cliches or accepted bits of "wisdom"
never were any good —
never were accurate and never worked.
Others were fine once
but simply don't fit with today.

This book seeks to *expose* a few of the old cliches
for what they are —
outdated philosophies or inaccurate insights
posing as wisdom.
Then it replaces the used-up notions
with some updated maxims —
little statements that reflect our world as it really is,
and our lifestyles as they really ought to be.

CLICHE: An old piece of hackneyed or stereotyped
"wisdom" which has become trite and meaningless.

Taken from the French "clicher" which refers to print-
ing from a metal plate which clamps down and repeat-
edly produces a stereotyped image.

MAXIM: A useful and practical catchphrase which states
a current truth in a way that gives insight and has a ben-
eficial influence on how we see things and how we do
things.

Taken from the Latin maxima propositio which means
"greatest statement" or a sound general truth.

CONTENTS

Preface 11
Prologue 17

PART ONE

Old Cliches and New Maxims
About Attitudes, Paradigms, and
Personal Management

INTERMISSION

PART TWO

Old Cliches and New Maxims
About Priorities, Relationships, and Families

It's not easy to challenge some of the best-known and oft-quoted cliches in the world — sayings that frequently seem to carry within them the wisdom of the ages. It's difficult, and often unpopular, to disagree with any "traditional wisdom" — with notions or ideas that have become part of our collective way of thinking.

And it's downright dangerous to take on your mother-in-law, your college professor, your own father, and the time-management experts of the world — all at once — in a single little book.

But with due respect to them all, that's what this book does. Just as we can learn a lot about a particular time by studying its arts or its fashion, we can learn about ourselves by thinking about the cliches — the traditional and accepted wisdom — that most of us grew up with. And we can appreciate how fast our world is changing by realizing how much *alteration* some of these cliches need in order to serve us well in today's world.

I don't actually have anything personal against the old cliches. There's nothing inherently wrong with most of them. Many of them were once practical and wise — just as the people who coined them — just as the people who used them. (See ... I really don't want to argue with my mother-in-law.)

You see, it's not these sayings or those people who have changed. It's the *times* and the *circumstances* in which we live.

Some of the old cliches in this book simply *fit* better (and worked better) in an older time.

Please don't think that I'm suggesting or advocating a changing *morality*. Right and wrong do *not* change. There are values that are both universal and eternal. But circumstances and situations and options *do* change. And the world has never known a time when they were changing faster!

In days gone by, life was simpler, and so was wisdom. Separating everything into "things worth doing well" and "things not worth doing at all" worked better in a time with fewer options, fewer demands. Laziness was differently defined in a day when work was physical and "doing something" was always better than "sitting there." And the rule of "work before play" was perfectly practical when cows needed milking or work required daylight.

Today, in our stressful and complex lives, play sometimes needs prioritizing over work — and frequently the most productive thing we can do is "sit there" —

and there are a great many things that are worth doing, but just barely!

What we need in our new and more flexible world is a different set of paradigms — different ways of looking at life and at the art of living it — fresh maxims to live by.

We work a lot today on our *techniques* — on the methods by which we do things and on the tools and technology we use. "Improvement" is often thought of as a better invention, and "progress" as a better procedure. But real growth, real improvement, and real progress only happen when *attitudes* change, when we learn to change how we look at our situations and how we *think* about our lives.

It is our attitudes that control what we see from day to day, what we put into our lives, and what we get out of them. And our attitudes are formed, to a rather amazing extent, by the little proverbs and platitudes that we accept as "truth." This is a book, then, about *changing our minds,* changing *how* we think and changing *what* we think of as "wisdom."

Each of the following chapters is titled and begun with the *old cliche* and then concluded with the *new maxim*. In most cases I think you will find that the old saying prompts feelings of worry or guilt, while the new one frees and energizes. I've been rather personal (maybe dangerously so) in attributing the old cliches to the people in my own life who "used them on me," and I've tried to explain my own changing attitudes through personal experiences that I hope parallel your own.

So . . . with advance acknowledgments and peace offerings to moms, dads, teachers, coaches, employers, advisers, bumper stickers, and all of yesterday's cliches, let's look for some new sayings that help us make sense of today and maybe (for a little while) of tomorrow.

PART ONE

Old Cliches and New Maxims About Attitudes, Paradigms, and Personal Management

IF A THING IS WORTH DOING, IT'S WORTH DOING WELL.

My father used to say it to me — often. And he lived it! We built a log cabin one summer. Mostly my dad built it — with what he graciously called "help" from my eight-year-old brother and ten-year-old me.

"Pull the nail out if it bends — don't just bash it over and start a new nail. Pull it out and straighten it and pound it in straight." It didn't matter if it was in a place no one would ever see. "If a thing is worth doing, it's worth doing well."

When my brother and I had our paper routes, the paper was supposed to be on the porch, not on the steps or in the driveway, and there was a huge difference between a "good" report card with B's and a "great" one with A's.

I remember once when I wanted another job besides the paper route. Dad said, "Don't bite off more than you can chew. Don't start something you can't finish; don't do it at all if you can't do it well!"

So what's changed? Well-built houses, good grades, and papers on the porch are all still good ideas.

What's changed is the *pace* at which we live — and the sheer number of options and demands we face.

My wife, Linda, dropped off a neighbor child one day and went in with him to say hello to his mother. His mother is a busy young professional who is trying to balance her career with her household and with the raising of her three young children.

On this particular day she was working on a cake that was so fancy that Linda assumed it was a wedding cake. "Who's getting married?" she asked.

"Oh, no one," said our neighbor with a laugh. "The church is just having a social and they asked me to bring a cake."

"Whew," responded Linda. "Why such an elaborate one, with all you have to do? You must love to make cakes!"

"I hate it, actually" said our friend. *"But I was always taught that if a thing is worth doing, it's worth doing well!"*

The silliness of the cliche in that particular situation struck Linda and our friend at that moment and they had a good laugh.

"What I should have done," the neighbor concluded, *"is bought an unfrosted cake at the supermarket, frosted it for the church social, and put it on an elaborate cake stand."*

In an increasingly complex world, some things are less "black and white" in terms of being worth doing well or not worth doing at all. There are things worth reading, but not carefully or exhaustively. There are places worth only a quick visit. There are some tasks and obligations that we ought to tend to, but with minimum effort and exertion. There are TV channels worth having but not worth watching very often. There are people we can meet without feeling that we must become close friends. There are more and more things worth doing but not worth killing ourselves over. And trying to do everything *well* is a sure recipe for stress.

So . . . there are *three* categories that we need to learn to recognize:

FIRST, the relatively small number of things that are truly *worth doing well*. A good way to recognize them is to ask the question, Will this matter in five years?

SECOND: There are a huge number of things not worth doing at all — and ridding ourselves of them can bring a stress-reducing simplicity into our lives.

FINALLY, there is the important-to-recognize middle category — things that are just barely worth doing. It is this third category that leads us to a new maxim:

IF A THING IS JUST BARELY WORTH DOING, THEN JUST BARELY DO IT.

Being able to categorize the pressures, demands, opportunities, and options of life into these three groups is perhaps the most basic key to balance and the most basic escape from stress. Once these three categories are defined, recognized, and mentally *used*, the *guilt* of not doing everything perfectly disappears and is replaced by a kind of pleasant pride in *saving* ourselves (by slacking off on the "hardly worth doings") *for* the things that are worth doing well.

NEVER PUT OFF UNTIL TOMORROW
WHAT YOU CAN DO TODAY.

It was my maternal grandmother who taught me this one — and taught it, and taught it. "Do it now." "Don't procrastinate." "Get it done."

There were a lot of these shorter variations on the theme, but her favorite was the full-blown and more philosophical-sounding "Never put off until tomorrow what you can do today."

"You can't even enjoy yourself when you go out to play," she would say, "if you've got work that isn't finished." The funny thing was I *could* enjoy myself, until she came out to drag me back to finish my job.

No one could ever call Grandma a hypocrite. She herself never put off *anything*. She had a big household and garden, a lot to do, and she lived after the time of live-in help and before the time of modern labor-saving devices. She also had a "church job." She also worked in the community.

I loved my grandmother. I still do, and I appreciate the work ethic she taught me — an ethic that never changes. What *has* changed is the *type* of work most of us do, and the *need* we have for spontaneity and flexibility.

I worked in Honolulu between my sophomore and junior years of college. One weekend I made my way to the big island of Hawaii, and was trying to hitchhike from Kona, on the west coast, to Hilo, on the east. It was nearly a full day's journey then, and I assumed I'd need several different rides to make it.

The first car that stopped for me was a beat-up, chugging old vehicle containing a wonderful native Hawaiian couple who introduced themselves as Rusty and Honey. "Where you go?" they inquired in pigdin English.

"I'm headed for Hilo," I responded.

All day long they drove me through the interior of the island, stopping frequently to show me a waterfall or a par-

ticularly beautiful bit of jungle. They took delight in my inter-est. They were like children sharing their toys. Their spon-taneity and joy were contagious, and I found myself having a wonderful time.

As the sun set behind us, we pulled into Hilo and I thanked them for a great day, adding that I surely felt lucky that the first car that stopped for me was going all the way to Hilo.

"Oh, we weren't going to Hilo," Rusty said.

"What — where were you going?"

"To the grocery store," said Honey, matter-of-factly.

I guess the confused look on my face was a question, and Rusty answered it with words that I'll never forget: "We can go to grocery store tomorrow, but can't drive you to Hilo tomorrow."

Most of us are not as carefree as Rusty and Honey. We live in a world where spontaneity and spur-of-the-moment opportunities seem in short supply. But if we examine life closely, there are often things that really can be put off without damage or detriment. (Putting off writing a memo or not quite finishing a sales report doesn't always have the same kind of predictable nega-tive natural consequences as not milking a cow or fail-ing to gather the eggs or cover the haystack before a storm.) Many things today can, and sometimes should, be put off! Even the IRS has an "automatic extension."

Procrastination can become a terrible habit; but, used selectively, it can actually be a great *technique* for helping us prioritize what really matters and for opening up our tight little lives to the joy of the moment, to the needs of others, to the serendipity and "happy surprises" that can be a part of our lives if we look for and welcome them.

Think about:

• A father, working hard at a project in his office, who looks out the window and notices the first warm and windy afternoon of spring — and decides to put off his work until tomorrow so that he can go fly a kite with his six-year-old today.

• A manager who is trying to finish her "to do" list for the morning and is interrupted by a phone call from an old acquaintance who is between flights at the airport. She decides to put off the rest of her list and to go to the airport and renew the acquaintance.

• A dutiful, do-it-yourself husband who is using a rare free evening to repaint the guest bedroom. As he rolls the paint, he's thinking about his wife and how long it has been since they've been out alone together. He hears the garage open and realizes she's home from her meeting earlier than she'd predicted. He decides to set the paint roller down and takes his wife to a movie instead.

Notice, in each incident, the word "*decides.*" When we see an opportunity to do something *right now* that can't be done later and make a *decision* to put off what can be put off in favor of what can't (even if the thing we put off is *work* and the thing we do instead is a bit frivolous or silly) — when we do this, we are *using* rather than abusing the technique of *selective procrastination*.

Maybe we'll feel better about that technique if we have a new maxim for it — that way we'll feel *wise* when we do it rather than slothful.

ALWAYS PUT OFF A "PUT-OFFABLE" IN FAVOR OF A "NOW OR NEVER."

Carve those words in the granite of your psyche, and perhaps the next time you "purposefully procrastinate," you can mentally pat yourself on the back instead of feeling your long-departed grandmother kick you in the backside.

WORK BEFORE PLAY.

You guessed it — my mother! This one is an all-time favorite of mothers everywhere, and naturally so — it couldn't be any other way.

In my boyhood, in the vacant middle of our city block, my neighborhood friends and I created a baseball diamond. The back screen consisted of two discarded old sets of bed springs, bases of big flat rocks (tough to slide into) and the field itself of tall grass cut down by my best friend's new power rotary mower (the first on the block). The base paths were made simply by so many sneakers running them so often.

Anyway — I was always trying to get to that ball field and Mom was always saying, "Work before play." And there was always some work to be done. She could think of a hundred ideas for work without a moment's notice. Doing some more work somewhere was always my "ticket" to go and play.

Looking back, of course, I know I learned that the lesson of work is the lesson of life, and my mother, partly with her three-word cliche, taught it to me. I didn't need to learn to play — I had great natural aptitude for that. I needed to learn to work.

The interesting irony of today is that many of us are extremely good at work, and disciplined and dedicated to it — and very bad at play. We have little aptitude for play, little ability at it, and we need to *relearn* the joy, the refreshment, the relaxation and the restoration of *play*.

We spend some family time each summer at a pristine mountain lake. The kids love the beach and the water, and we love the peace and the quiet time to write and to read.

Most of the beach houses and cabins near ours are frequented by their owners only on weekends. People drive in on Friday night and leave on Sunday. What's interesting to observe is how hard it is for most of them to start relaxing. We see them up early on Saturday—painting, clipping, mowing, or polishing boats that too often never even get put in the water. Many enjoy this work — since it's a change from their usual weekday work — but there also seems to be a certain habit *in their labor, a pattern and a certain comfortable familiarity in working and an awkward unfamiliarity in any kind of play. Once in a while you see someone working at play, trying to remember how to do it and how to enjoy it.*

Another thing that happens at this summer place is my own interaction between work and play. With my mother's motto still in my ears I often get up and, since writing is my work, resolve to finish a certain number of pages before I go to the beach or to the tennis court. Or Linda reminds me that there is a fence to be mended or a deck to be painted and that I ought to get it done.

But an interesting element enters the picture. There are certain brief periods, often early in the day, when the lake is as still and perfect as a piece of glass — times when water skiing can take on an almost mystical quality of smoothness and beauty. And there are other moments when an offshore breeze sweeps gently across the lake, making it perfect for windsurfing. The kids say, "Dad, we need to go now!" And if I say, "Work before play," they say, "We'll miss the moment."

Here's the startling revelation: I work best after I play. My mind is clearer, my thoughts quicker, my writing more like I want it to be.

What is playing anyway? A form of learning? An avenue of pleasure and joy? An exercise of body or senses? Is there something inherently inferior or less noble in play when it is compared to work?

In today's world the *nature* of work and play have changed. Much of our work is mental work, and it is *enhanced* and *improved* by intermittent periods of rejuvenating play. It used to be that most work was physical and tiring — so play was often passive and physically lazy. Now our work often leaves us mentally tired and physically unused, unstretched, unimproved.

And the aggressive, competitive, comparative nature of our work lives puts us in a work habit that clutches us and compels us to be doing some kind of "productive work" even when we're "relaxing." We relegate play to too late in the day, when we're too tired, when the glass is gone off the lake and the chance for real and spontaneous fun is gone.

When we lose our ability to play, we also lose our *playfulness* and a certain amount of our humor, our flexibility, and our spontaneity is sucked away with it.

Perhaps, in this work-oriented, work-obsessed world, we need a new maxim:

STALE WORK IS RENEWED
BY FRESH PLAY.

We took a business associate to our lake for a long weekend one summer. He spent the first day worrying about the calls he couldn't make since we had no phone. The second day he gave in a little and started relaxing and enjoying himself. At the end of the third day he said, "You know, I think I've forgotten how to play." Then a pause and smile. "But I'm starting to think I have a natural aptitude for it and can relearn it if I just apply myself."

DON'T JUST SIT THERE,
DO SOMETHING!

This is an especially touchy chapter because it was my mother-in-law who always said this one.

"Don't just sit there, do something." Now, don't misunderstand. She liked me . . . she still likes me, I hope. She will still like me after she reads this book, I think. She didn't single me out for the advice. She said it to everyone. "Be up and doing!" "Get off your duff!" "Be active!" "Don't let any moss grow under your feet!" Even "An idle mind is the devil's workshop." And she said it by example as well as with words. If there was ever anyone more active than my grandmother, it is my mother-in-law. Sitting down is just not part of her modus operandi. She is eighty-five as I write this and can still beat me at bowling! (Or weeding a garden or practically anything else we ever happen to do together.)

Well, it *is* better to be "up and doing" than to be down and drooping. No question. Always has been, always will be.

But something *has* changed! We have evolved into a society where there is so *much* going on that we are *always* acting and doing, sometimes at the expense of thinking and feeling.

In a less urban, less mechanized, less complex and competitive time, there were natural seasons and periods of reflection and repose. There were natural "breaks" after the planting or after the harvest, and when it got dark at night, work was done.

Not so today! We may have business cycles, but none of them involve rest. We have weekends, but they're usually the time to do the work we couldn't get to during the week. And we have evenings, but the night belongs to homework with the kids, or to working overtime, or to trying to "play as hard as we work."

One evening, after a particularly long and hectic day, I was eating a late meal by myself in the kitchen and over-hearing Linda's discussion in the living room with our four-teen-year-old son, Josh.

He was saying that he'd had a tough day, too, starting with his five A.M. paper route and two tests in school. Linda was reminding him that his piano lesson was tomorrow and he hadn't practiced — and that the dishwasher (his job) was still unemptied. He was telling his mother that he had some math homework to do and he had to finish a scout merit-badge requirement before next week's Court of Honor, but that the most important basketball game of the year was going into the second half on TV. He also mentioned that he'd promised his friend, Chad, that he'd go over and see his new computer game.

Linda, being my mother-in-law's daughter, offered her usual advice, but in her frustration with her own and her son's busyness, it came out backward:

"Well, don't just do something — sit there!"

I went in and joined them for a good laugh, but as our amusement subsided, we realized that under the circum-stances, the reversed cliche was better advice than the original.

Josh had more to do than he possibly could do that night (just as most of us have more to do than we can most of the time), and rather than just doing something, what he need-

ed to do was to sit there *for a few minutes and* decide *what mattered most or* figure out *some way to get some things done now and some later.*

We sometimes let ourselves get infected with the notion that any action is preferable to any inaction, that *doing* is superior to *thinking*, that doing something — anything — is better than occasionally doing nothing at all so we can sit and think instead.

In a world where there is an endless number of things to do, we can become fanatic, frantic whirlwinds of activity, working ourselves to an exhausted frazzle each day and yet looking back over the weeks and months and not being able to see much progress. Like someone sawing furiously with a dull saw, we keep *doing something* and tire and stress ourselves, never taking time to just *sit there* and sharpen our saw.

We need the new maxim that Linda coined by the slip of her tongue:

DON'T JUST DO SOMETHING, SIT THERE!

Sit there long enough each morning to decide what is really important during the day ahead. Sit there long enough once or twice during the day to *collect* your thoughts, to meditate for a moment, to calm your mind and regain perspective. Sit there on a child's bed once in a while at bedtime and just listen to him. Sit there and watch a sunset rather than just doing something.

Thoughtful "sitting there" is rapidly becoming a lost art, stomped out by trying to do something every minute.

Reversing this old cliche in our minds can give us a new maxim that slows us down, tunes us in, and makes us more selective and more purposeful in the things we choose to do.

GET SERIOUS!

This one still rings in my ears! In the deep, loud voice of my high school basketball coach. To him basketball was life — and life was very serious. "Come on!" "Think!" "Don't make that same mistake again!" "Set that pick like you mean it!" "You're not here to fool around!" "Get serious!"

The irony of talking like this about something that was supposed to be fun never occurred to him. Once in exasperation he even said, "What do you guys think this is, a *game*?"

Well it *was* a game, of course — and a game that is better played when people are loose rather than tense, axed and enjoying themselves rather than pressured and overtrying.

Life, while it is much more than a game, works in much the same way.

Most of us take ourselves far too seriously. We turn life into a fierce competition by comparing ourselves not only with real people but with the unreal images and expectations of the media. Leisure gets as serious and competitive as anything else. We have to *win*, or at least improve, otherwise what would be the point? We plan serious vacations (right down to the minute) so that we can maximize our time off. We tell our children to "get serious" at the very time they are enjoying themselves most. And we trick ourselves into thinking that seriousness is synonymous with success.

"What do you guys do for fun?"

It was a strange way to start a sophisticated business seminar. And it looked *strange too — the casual, bearded speaker, dressed in cords and a flannel shirt, talking to an audience clad in serious dark suits with patterned power ties.*

But that was how he began. He and I were the two featured speakers at a corporate "personal renewal" conference. I was seated on the stand, behind the speaker, watching the audience.

"You guys look pretty serious to me," my counterpart said. "What do you do to relax?"

The audience looked a little confused, some a bit irritated. They were here for serious renewal! *What was this? Finally someone raised his hand. "I play tennis."*

"Elaborate," said the speaker.

"Well, I'm up to a four-point-five ranking and I got to the club semifinals this spring. . . ." It was quickly obvious that this guy's tennis was serious — even stressful.

For ten more minutes the speaker tried to get someone to come up with something simple and spontaneous and fun. Finally he started telling his own ways of loosening up and enjoying the day-to-day. He told some of the crazy little things he did to lighten his business travel: paying the toll at toll booths for the car behind him and watching the surprised reaction in his rearview mirror. Putting little "dot" stickers up in the curve of an airplane window or a public rest-room mirror so that if he was ever there again, he could remember he'd been there before. Starting conversations with total strangers. Paying restaurant bills anonymously for people who looked like they couldn't afford it.

By now the faces in the audience showed a mixture of skepticism and real envy — as they realized that his message was simply that what we need to renew ourselves is not to do more *but to* relax *more.*

I love to coach six- and seven-year-olds. Our city has a program called Biddy Basketball with a lower basket and smaller basketballs — and without scoreboards. I learned in my first year of coaching that the kids don't respond very well or improve very much from criticism. Telling them not to double-dribble or pointing out their errors just causes very serious and worried looks on their little faces — and their technique actually gets worse.

What does work is to praise them and to have fun. Every time any of them do *anything* even remotely promising, I tell them how well they did. The others listen, watch, emulate. And before each practice or game we have a standard question and answer. "Why are we playing basketball?" "To have fun!"

Life of course has its serious side. But why "serious-ize" the parts that don't have to be? Part of our seriousness is habit. Just as "lightening up" can become a counterhabit.

A *sense* of humor is well named. A sense is something that can be developed. As you try consciously to be more aware, to *notice* the amusing, ironic, or humorous aspects of everyday life, you sensitize yourself to the lighter side and learn to laugh more — particularly at yourself.

And *lightness* is an intriguing and multimeaningful

word. As we choose a lighter approach and attitude, we shed the somber heaviness and pessimism of seriousness and brighten with wider awareness and clearer insight. "Lightness" is the opposite of darkness as well as of heaviness.

G. K. Chesterton said it best, and though his quotation is now old, it can become a new maxim for today:

THE REASON ANGELS CAN FLY IS THAT THEY HAVE LEARNED TO TAKE THEMSELVES LIGHTLY.

In our families we need to remember that *"crisis* plus *time* usually equals *humor."* Like the time that seven of our children spilled their milk at the same dinner, or the late-night return from a camping trip when we didn't have a house key and had to camp one more night — in the backyard.

In our work life we need to remember that most of the hassles and small failures aren't remembered — by others or by ourselves.

Properly viewed, people are essentially interesting and amusing. And life is essentially beautiful and entertaining. And we ourselves are often pretty funny.

ACT, DON'T RE-ACT.

This one was a favorite of a professor of mine, at the Harvard Business School no less. He was a John Houseman type of character with a slow, gravelly voice and heavy-lidded eyes that looked right through you. I almost expected him to say, "Make money the old-fashioned way . . . earrrrrrn it!" But what he *did* say was:

"Act, don't re-act!"

"Never be surprised. If you are surprised, it means you didn't preparrrrrre well enough, you didn't do enough contingency plannnnnning."

"Be in controoooool . . . be in charrrrrrge . . . act, don't re-act."

He was one of my favorite professors, so it took me

years to realize that his motto was ridiculous, that it actually caused stress and frustration and put a damper on all kinds of joy and spontaneity.

———

"Act, don't re-act" may have some limited, narrow application in certain business situations where you want to stay on your own agenda and stick with your own strategy. But in *life*, where the constant is *surprise* the motto becomes a joke. Things happen every day to which we need to *respond*. *Surprise* is another name for opportunity. The faster our world moves, the more important our ability to respond and react becomes.

In families some of us have noticed that children have a fascinating knack of *always* needing us at the most inconvenient time. And just try saying, "This is not a good time, let me pencil you in for three-thirty tomorrow so that I can think of a strategy and can act rather than re-act." It simply won't work. Children need us when they need us, and the best time to answer them is when they ask!

Friends call at unexpected times. Sunsets surprise us. Ideas come along at random times. Circumstances change. Unpredictables — from the weather to the market to our own metabolism — surprise us and dwell inside us. What a world in which to say, "Act, don't re-act." What pretension even to imagine that we control enough to make our days always unfold according to our plans or lists.

———

We once gave a seminar to a group of business people and challenged them to make their "action lists" on the left-hand side of their planning page and then draw a line down the center and leave the right side blank to symbolize the possibility of unexpected opportunity, needs, or spontaneous ideas that might come into their lives, unplanned and unexpected.

Then we redefined the perfect day — not as one in which everything got checked off the list but as one in which at least two or three things came along that were better or more important or more timely than what they had planned. Serendipitous things, things they would re–act to rather than act on, things they would do instead of what they had planned, things they would write down after the fact on the right side of their pages.

We challenged them to be observant enough to notice the unplanned, unexpected things — and to be flexible enough to appreciate them, even to relish the surprises rather than resent them.

After one week we met again for debriefing. We analyzed what was written on the right-hand side. Ideas, new acquaintances, beauty observed, spontaneous time with children, unexpected problems that were dealt with.

We analyzed the planned things that didn't *get done on the left side* because *of the "interruptions" on the right. Some were rescheduled, some were "caught up on" later in the day. And some were simply forgotten because they weren't that important or because the surprises or "serendipities" on the right superseded them or made them unnecessary.*

The most interesting lesson came when we asked the participants where the greatest value was *— left or right. We asked them if they had to throw away everything they had made happen on the left (the planned, listed activities) or to throw out everything that had happened to them on the right, which would they hang on to?*

After some thinking and comparing, everyone said that *if they had to choose, they would keep the right — the ideas, beauty, relationships, opportunities, needs — things they reacted to rather than the "thing" things that they acted upon.*

But life *isn't* a choice between acting and reacting. We all do a lot of both. In a well-lived life each side complements the other. It is the goals and plans we have that give us a direction and a track to run on. The challenge is to see more than the track, it is to see both sides *and* down the line. We need to cast off the blinders and *notice* the unexpected. We need to relish rather than resist surprise and to add flexibility to discipline and spontaneity to structure. Let the right enhance the left. Get the creative, poetic right side of the brain to work as well as the logical, strategic left. Remodel the old cliche about acting and not reacting so that it reads:

ACT AND RESPOND.

In basketball (and most other sports) a good defense causes offensive opportunities, and a strong offense makes the defense more effective, more natural. In life, clear goals and the offense of "acting" can enhance, contrast, and complement our defense of responding and reacting well to events and circumstances we did not plan.

The concept of *serendipity* is a bridge that can span and connect our actions and reactions. Serendipity, defined by Horace Walpole, who coined the word, is a state of mind and of awareness by which one consistently discovers something good while seeking something else. A serendipitous attitude, in other words, is

one in which a person *acts* on his goals, plans, and directions, but *with* an awareness and flexible attitude that
allows him to notice, respond, and *react* to unexpected
needs and opportunities along the way.

HURRY UP

I was trying to think who it was that always used to say this one to me — and I realized that it was *everyone*. Teachers tell us to hurry up. Parents tell us to hurry up. Employers tell us to hurry up. And perhaps most of all, we tell ourselves to hurry up.

Hurry is an interesting word. There is a certain stressfulness even in the *sound* of it. Maybe it sounds a little like "harried" or "hassled." It implies a certain lack of control or composure, a bit of desperation, and at least a little fatigue.

So why are we always telling each other, and telling ourselves, to "hurry up"? "Well," we tell ourselves, "there's a lot to do, and 'if you stop you rust,' or 'grass grows under your feet.' "

Ponder the interesting fact that people seldom hurry when they really know what they're doing. Someone who is confident, who has thought everything through and knows quite clearly what he or she wants to do and how to do it — such a person usually seems efficient, sure, unhurried. And, amazingly, these people seem to get more done than people in a hurry.

I came home late one evening — too late. There had been an incredible amount to do at the office, and I had been try- ing to hurry through it all and get home in time to have din- ner with Linda and the children. The more I rushed, the faster time seemed to pass and the more it seemed I had to do.

When I finally got home, dinner was long over and the children were asleep in bed. I slipped into their room and sat down in the rocking chair, watching their sweet faces in peace- ful sleep, chastising myself for prioritizing things at the office above getting home in time to play with them.

As I sat there in silence, I was startled by an intermittent clicking sound behind me. My eyes followed the sound, adjusted to the dim light, and I watched the little fuzzy ger- bil in his cage, running full speed but staying in the same place in the whirring cylinder of his treadmill. That's me, I thought, *running full tilt, hurrying all day, and, finding myself in the same place as when I started.*

The analogy kept going in my mind. The faster we run, the faster the world around us seems to move. Time itself seems to speed up as we hurry, so that, like the gerbil in the treadmill, we get no farther by going fast than by walking slow.

We think of time as an absolute — as something always passing at exactly the same rate. We measure it in calibrated seconds, minutes, and hours on our clocks and in uniform days and weeks on our calendars. But it's not that simple or that linear. Sometimes our hurry makes it pass faster, and once in a while our calmness makes it slow down and it seems that we have time for everything.

There, that evening in the darkened room of my sleeping children, I resolved to reject the adage of hurrying up and to seek instead the illusive but quite wonderful phenomenon of "the speed of going slow."

A Christian minister friend of mine once told me that God is never referred to in Scripture as being in a hurry or in haste. Christ always had time, even for insignificant individuals. Satan, on the other hand, is often depicted as hurrying — "rushing to and fro in the earth."

There are of course times to hurry, situations that

require haste. The problem today is that hurry has become the rule rather than the exception, the norm rather than the occasional need. A steady diet of hurry produces stress and, as in the gerbil syndrome, seems to make time speed up so that we find ourselves understanding the words of the old farmer who had moved to the faster pace of the city, "The hurrier I go, the behinder I get."

One who has perfected a calmer, slower, more peaceful pace can *enjoy* an occasional rush or hurry — it is for him a refreshing change of pace, an exciting challenge. I thought about this the other day as I rowed my slender racing skull on the glass-smooth water of Bear Lake in Idaho. The sun was setting, the lake's surface looked like gold, and I sliced through its stillness with easy, slow pulls on the oars. With rowing, especially over a long distance, you go smoother and faster when the strokes are long and even. Trying to hurry throws the symmetry — one oar breaks before the other or slices too deep, and you are thrown off your straight course. Too much haste makes your course jerky and erratic, and there is frustration in your stroke rather than the smooth pleasure of rhythm. But with the pace controlled and smooth, you are ready to double-time your stroke and maximize your speed for short bursts when another boat challenges you or when you close in on a finish line.

Life is similar. A purposeful but peaceful pace rests us, makes us more aware and sensitive, and makes our hurry moments, when they do come, exciting rather than fatiguing.

An article that I happened to read in a dentist's waiting room attempted to diagnose all the problems of modern, Western man in two words: "Too much." We try to possess too much, we have too many options that are too complex, and most of all we try to do too much. In the process there is too little time to *think*, too little energy left to *enjoy*.

There are other old cliches that seek to counter the antiwisdom of the phrase *hurry up*. I like and believe the one that says, "Haste makes waste" as well as the one that says, "Take time to smell the roses."

But I think we need a new maxim, one that refers to the power we have to actually slow time down, to find *more* time by prioritizing better, by not doing so many unimportant or marginally important things. The maxim is essentially the discovery I made that night while watching my children's faces and their gerbil's treadmill:

SEEK THE SPEED OF GOING SLOW.

When our motto is "hurry up," there is always *too much* of things, of jobs, of obligations — and too little time. When we slow down, think more, and prioritize better, we begin to find the deceptive speed of going slow and focus on fewer things and find we have more time.

PLAN YOUR WORK
AND WORK YOUR PLAN.

My first boss always said, "Plan your work and work your plan." He was a disciple of detailed planning. He had other cliches too — all related. "He who fails to plan, plans to fail." "A goal without a plan is only a wish."

Many of the cliches in this book need to be exploded, dismantled, and discarded; but this one only needs a little alteration and a few caveats.

Certainly work needs planning, and certainly planning needs follow-through. But when planning becomes too detailed or too set, it may work against the very *flexibility* and *serendipity* that we need in a fast-changing, unpredictable world. And it may remove the spontaneity and responsiveness that sometimes lead us to our finest thoughts and most productive actions.

My first personal clue to some kind of "countertruth" that balanced or modified the idea of exhaustive preparation or planning came to me quite by chance several years ago. I was an aggressive young professional who had quite logically decided that I had so much to do that careful prioritizing and detailed planning were my only hopes. I had developed a ritual of getting up early each Sunday morning, setting some weekly goals, and then planning all the "steps" I would take during the week to reach those goals.. I'd been doing this planning religiously every Sunday morning for several months.

Then one Sunday, just as I had finished writing down my goals for the week — and before I'd started planning how I'd reach the goals or scheduling my time — an unexpected phone call came in, and I ended up spending most of the morning on the phone dealing with a problem. Then things just got busy, and I never got back to the planning.

As the week unfolded, I was very aware of the goals I'd set, but didn't have my usual detailed plans. Yet interestingly and, I thought, surprisingly, I found at the end of the week that I had reached the goals I had set. I'd just done things as they occurred to me or as the opportunity arose or the thought struck rather than following a schedule or a list.

Simply stated, goals are more important than plans. If a goal is clear and we are committed to it, we'll probably find a way to reach it. And sometimes that "way" will be more sensitive, better tuned, and more direct if we're open and flexible and watching for opportunities than if we're rigid and locked into some specific plan and schedule that we *thought* was the best way or the best time to get it done.

Whoa, careful, wait, don't misinterpret! This is not a case or a plea for no planning or no preparation. Rather, it is an observation that overpreparation or too-detailed plans can make us less *responsive* and sometimes less creative and opportunistic. Goals without plans or with fairly general plans have an interesting kind of *power*. We seem to move toward them almost subconsciously, as though they were magnets that pull on us and on our circumstances.

The best speeches are often the unwritten ones where one responds to the feel of an audience. The best ideas often come as flashes of insight rather than the culmination of a long analysis. The best moves are sometimes made on the spur of the moment. (Michael Jordan said he decided what to do with the basketball *after* he had left the ground and was soaring through the air.)

Good, committed goals have a power of their own, and they can sometimes be smothered or weighted down by too many highly specific and carefully laid plans that may "stiffen us up" and block out spontaneous opportunities.

Hence the new maxim:

BE FIRM ON THE GOAL, BUT FLEXIBLE ON THE PLAN.

A wise, elderly friend of mine — a very creative and unique individual — once used a mathematical metaphor to express this thought. He said that we learn to do basic sums and timetables as children, but that as we get older and more confident, we want more creative mathematics — new approaches, new discoveries. Planning a rigid "one-way" approach to a goal we have is like using laborious, predictable hand calculations in math. Having a goal and constantly looking for a new and better way to reach it (or even for a new and higher goal) is a more-advanced and *fun* level of thinking.

A CHANGE IS AS GOOD AS A REST.

Well . . . there is some truth in this one and in other related cliches. Variety *is* the spice of life. People and perspectives *are* renewed by change. Routine *can* be so tiresome that anything that breaks it can be helpful.

But as good as a rest? Interchangeable with rest? Don't you believe it.

Rest should be more than a necessity. It can be a pleasure, a reward, even a kind of an art in that some people get very good at it while most of us don't do it very well at all.

One reason people used to be better at resting, at sleeping, at *releasing* the concerns and activities of the day is that there used to be times when there wasn't anything else to do. Evenings and Sundays and other traditional times of rest were relatively free of activity and, if we go back a generation or two, even free of media. Now we're always linked in, able to work, able to shop, able to "spectate," recreate, commiserate, speculate. Nothing stops, nothing closes, there is no down time. Sundays are the most consuming days of recreation; evenings are when we socialize or catch up on what needs to be done at home since we haven't been there all day. And vacations are often so intense that we need a rest when we get home.

Several years ago I was doing some writing on traditional values and age-honored standards, such as the Ten Commandments. I became intrigued that eight of the ten are "shalt nots" — things we're told not to do. The two that are stated positively were especially interesting to me: "Honor thy parents" (because we were writing parenting books) and "Remember the Sabbath day" (because I was concerned and thinking a lot about my own personal need for rest).

The ancient idea of "sabbatical" — the notion of taking not only every seventh day but every seventh year as a time of rest, reflection, and planning, seemed on the one hand so outdated and impractical yet on the other hand so appealing and needed.

I was also struggling at the time to find a planning or time-

management system that would work for me. I had a very large, very detailed Day-Timer book where I was trying to list and prioritize every daily task, appointment, and objective. It was taking a lot of my time to plan my time, and I was getting the feeling that my big planner and all my lists were managing me rather than the other way around.

As I studied about the ancient use of the Sabbath day, I was struck by the advantages of conceptual "goal and role"–oriented weekly planning over cluttered, list-oriented daily planning.

I threw away the huge planner and started spending an hour or so each Sunday just thinking about the most important things I could do during the week ahead in my three key roles of (a) husband, father, friend; (b) management consultant; and (c) thirty-five-year-old trying to take care of my own body and mind. I discovered that when I saved my Sundays for going to church and resting at home, I slipped into a calmer, slower rhythm that allowed me to see my life and its priorities more clearly. I found that when I shifted from "What do I have to do today?" to "What do I choose to do during the week ahead for family, for work, and for self?" I felt less stress and frustration and more strength and control. I also found that during the week opportunities or channels seemed to appear to do the things I had decided on Sunday were important.

Human beings are renewable, rechargeable devices. When we run down and don't rest, we being to lose our light, our sight, our might. Each person needs to find his own formula for rest, but it should not be thought of as an interruption or a grudged necessity, and certainly not as a waste of time. Rather, rest should be enjoyed, looked forward to, and planned for. For some, exercise is the best way to relax, and it brings on real rest. For others, rest is as simple as catching up on sleep. Sleep itself is different for different people. Some need a certain amount each night. Some do fine on less if they can take a nap or a rest in the afternoon or early evening. Some can catch up on weekends. The important thing is to *value* rest, to plan it, to relish it.

So . . . let's change a few words in the old cliche and turn it into a much-needed maxim.

NOTHING IS AS GOOD (OR AS NECESSARY) AS REAL REST.

Rested minds and bodies are able to truly re-create—to think about who they are and who they are becoming, to look backward as well as forward and think a little about where they've been as well as where they're going.

A rested body renews itself and is more likely to stay free from illness, and a rested mind not only resists stress and depression, it is more receptive to intuition, to little "nudges" or impressions or possibilities and to a clearer sense of priorities.

YOU MADE YOUR BED,
NOW LIE IN IT.

This one was said to me, with considerable conviction, by a well-meaning business associate. I was preparing to leave the consulting firm I had helped build because I wanted to change my focus and spend more time writing.

"Let me give you a little advice that you haven't asked for but that you sure do need," said my older colleague. "You don't just walk away from a profession you've spent years learning. You don't try to change course in mid-stream. You'll be starting from ground zero. You're too old a dog to learn new tricks. You're doing fine. You've invested a lot to be where you are. You've made your bed, now lie in it."

"It's a rut I'm in, not a bed," I tried to explain, "and I'm not even sure I made it. It was pretty much made by circumstance and things that just happened."

———

This old cliche is great as long as its intent is to remind us that we need to keep commitments and to accept the consequences of our actions and choices. But when it starts to mean "Stay what you are . . . don't change . . . don't risk . . . be satisfied . . . you can only be what you are now," it becomes limiting and counter-productive.

My colleague, advising against a career move, was advocating the low-risk status quo over the high-risk of change. "You've made your bed, now lie in it" was his way of saying "Don't leave your comfort zone."

What he didn't realize was that I *needed* to leave that comfort zone. A more useful cliche for me at that point in my life was "What doesn't *move* begins to *rust*."

Comfort imprisons more people than prison bars do, and I knew that it was time to move on. I understood that a well-conceived change has the power to expand both the quality and quantity of our lives! *Quality* because life becomes more interesting (the more we're challenged, the more awake we become). *Quantity* because changes seem to slow time down (compare how fast the weeks turn into years when you're in a routine with how wonderfully long and full a week seems when you're in a new place and experiencing new things).

———

Tennis has been important to me over the years because it's the one thing I do consistently to stay in shape. Tennis also seems to serve as a metaphor for life. Like life, it is such a mental game, and attitudes have so much to do with how well we do.

For years I had been dissatisfied with my backhand. I knew it was my weakness (as did everyone that I played). It had little of the top spin or the control or the confidence *of my forehand. I had tried several "adjustments" and had practiced endlessly hitting against a wall or a ball machine.*

One spring I decided that what I needed was not another adjustment or more practice but a whole new stroke.

I read articles, consulted a coach, and designed the heavier top-spin stroke I wanted. It required a completely different grip, a different back swing, even different footwork than what I had been using for twenty years. It felt foreign, difficult, awkward, and downright insecure. *But the alternative was to stay the same, to stay in my comfort zone, to fail to improve.*

I finally got it to where I could hit the way I wanted to in practice or with the ball machine, but in a match it was so much easier to revert to the old stroke.

Maybe you really can't teach an old dog new tricks, I would think. Maybe change really is too unpleasant, too risky, too hard. Maybe you do just have to lie in your bed once you've made it.

Still, hard as it was, I noticed that I was enjoying tennis more. It was different! *I was losing some points that I used to win, but I was winning some that I used to lose — and I was progressing, I was getting better.*

Teddy Roosevelt spoke with pity about the "cold and timid souls who have never known either victory or defeat" and with admiration of those "who were actually in the arena" . . . who try, who strive, who change.

"Multiple careers" is a notion that excites and intrigues people, but not all of them can make it happen. "Try something new" is a motto few dare to live by.

Comfort is the enemy.

Restlessness can be our ally.

The new maxim is:.

GET OUT OF YOUR BED
BEFORE IT GETS TOO COMFORTABLE.

Life is too long and too potentially wondrous to spend in one place, in one profession, in one interest. Commitments should be kept, most particularly those to family and to God. But we should have no commitment to rut or to routine.

KEYS YOUR NOSE TO THE GRINDSTONE.

Get it done! Don't stop! Get it over with! No interruptions! Get on to the next thing. Don't be distracted! Keep your eye on the ball! Keep your nose to the grindstone!

Ugh! What are you ever going to experience with your nose pressed up against that old stone? We drive ourselves, we push ourselves to work hard, and in the process we drive ourselves crazy and we drive past the joys and beauties too fast to really see them.

If we keep grinding away, where will it get us? Will we "get there"? To some mythical destination? To someplace that is better than where we are now? To the other side of the fence where the grass is greener?

To those who believe in a hereafter — in an eternity (and surveys show that 95 percent of us do) — *where is there*? Surely there is not some terminal, final destination, someplace where progress stops, where we stagnate and cannot ever go beyond.

If there is no full stop, no final end, if there's no quitting point or ultimate destination, then perhaps all life (this one and beyond) should be thought of not as a preface or run-up to something else, not as just the means to some other end, but as a long, even, unending *journey* where the point is not to finish or to arrive but to keep growing and progressing, and the goal is not to finally *get there* but to find *joy all along the way*.

I couldn't help noticing how opposite the two weekends were and how opposite their effects were on me. One weekend, keeping my nose to the grindstone, I went to a distant city, got some business done, and came home. The next weekend I accepted a friend's invitation to try hot-air ballooning. The first weekend I rode on jets because that was the fastest, most direct way to get exactly where I wanted to go. The second weekend we had no idea where we were going, because the wind and the air currents didn't tell us in advance.

The first weekend what I noticed was that the plane was late, my luggage was slow, and the meetings took longer than they should have. The second weekend I noticed the infinite loveliness of moving clouds, the patchwork quilt of the earth's fields and forests; the joy and company of my two fellow travelers, and a thousand other things.

The overriding purpose of the first weekend trip was to get somewhere and get the job done. The reason for the second weekend's trip was to enjoy the journey.

Jets versus hot-air balloons; fast, noisy snowmobiles versus slow, quiet cross-country skis; motorboats versus sailboats; Zig Zigler versus Thoreau.

Travel metaphors abound: the time snow closed the airport and we had to take the train over the Rockies from Salt Lake City to Denver — thirteen hours of exquisite, slow beauty instead of sixty-five minutes of fast boredom.

But real experience tells it better: *Taking* time to make a friend, *taking* time to notice, to enjoy, to smell roses and watch sunsets, *taking* time instead of *using* time to get there.

The new maxim for this chapter is completely obvious and not very new, but it's worth repeating:

ENJOY THE JOURNEY.

There is a phenomenon that's hard to explain through logic or by cause-and-effect. When we think more about the joy of the journey and less about the pressure of the destination, we get pretty much where we wanted to go anyway, and we arrive rested and relaxed.

THERE'S A TIME AND PLACE
FOR EVERYTHING.

The problem with this homey homily is that neither time nor place nor the people and circumstances that occupy them are completely within our control. Thinking they are — thinking we can control everything — leads to frustration and insensitivity.

Commercially, our delusions of control are called "time management" and include all kinds of products with tiresome names like day-timers, Filofax, time-extenders, and worst of all "Dayrunners."

Bad as all of these terms are, they're not as *dangerous* or as subtly deceitful as their computer-age cliche equivalent: "program your time."

Time *programming* seems to imply that time is like some sort of quantifiable data that can be manipulated, exactly and precisely located or stored, and used with precision and total control.

The problem is that we don't live in a vacuum and time is not *ours*. We move *through* it and while we have some control over what we do with it, it also has considerable control of us.

Of course we should take an active role in how we use our time and a deep interest in where we are going. But we should be more realistic about what we can and can't program.

Early in my career I took the time-programming approach to everything: work, family, even recreation. Two hours for this, fifteen minutes for that, all planned beforehand, all in "control."

I was frustrated quite often (more accurately, my plans were frustrated, which in turn frustrated me). I was frequently irritated that circumstances, and particularly other people didn't always go along with what I had programmed to happen. But I assumed that these difficulties were occurring simply because I had not yet perfected the science of time management.

I had a simple experience one week that started changing the direction of my thinking. I'd been too busy at the office to spend time with my six-year-old son, Josh, and I was beginning to feel guilty. Still, I'd found that guilt was easily relieved, or at least postponed, if you have a good day planner. I just found a free evening a week from Tuesday and penciled Josh in.

Alas, when next Tuesday rolled around, a minor crisis at the office kept me in the city late. But no problem, I hadn't told Josh of my plans anyway. I just crossed him off and put him down again for Thursday.

What I forgot was that Thursday was the last day of the month. As I prepared to leave the office to "carry out my goal" with Josh, the accountant rushed in with the monthly reports. Oh, well, shift Josh to the next Tuesday — at least I was planning something, at least my heart was in the right place.

The next Tuesday came and I did get away from work early. I even stopped at the toy store and got a model airplane that we could work on together. I bounced enthusiastically into the house and yelled for Josh. He didn't answer because he was engrossed in a TV program. I said "Josh, come on — I've got a model airplane, and we've got an hour to put it together." "Maybe later," he said. "I've got to see this show."

We can't program our children. We can't program other people. We can't program our circumstances. And we can't program our time.

What we can program is our attitudes. We can learn to respect and to respond to the unexpected twists and timings of the day. We can understand that there are teaching moments when our children are asking for our time and attention. We can realize that joy and insight and opportunity all come in moments and that those moments are not always convenient or pre-planned or exactly where we would like them to be.

The new maxim is:

KNOW WHEN *THIS* IS THE PLACE AND *NOW* IS THE TIME.

Especially in terms of relationships, *then* and *when* are important, but *now* is what really matters.

YOU ARE WHAT YOU EAT (OR WEAR, OR DRIVE, OR LIVE IN, OR DO)

The variations on this cliche are almost endless. We judge each other and we judge ourselves far too much by appearances, by "achievements," and by symbols of status. "The clothes make the man." "Your car says a lot about who you are." "You can't be better than you look." "Your job (or your title, or your address, or your resume) is your identity."

Nonsense. We know it's not true, but we behave and respond and think as though it were.

We live in a world where we concern ourselves too much with the "outer" and not enough with the "inner."

And the more judgmental and critical we become

(both of others and of ourselves), the more we are led into other related and equally untrue cliches such as "Winning isn't everything, it's the only thing."

For decades, in connection with our writing, Linda and I have lectured and spoken on goalsetting. Our whole approach took a dramatic turn as a result of one presentation we made on a winter weekend where we got some very interesting input and feedback from an audience.

It was a two-part, two-day presentation, and at the end of the day we asked everyone for a short list of three personal goals they had for the following year. That evening we sat in front of a fireplace and went through over two-hundred responses. As we did, something gradually became apparent. All of the goals had to do with things and with accomplishing. None of them (with the exception of a few diet or weight-loss objectives) had to do with becoming or with feeling. They were goals about achievements, not about relationships. They were about doing and getting, but not about being.

The next day we asked the audience to indicate, by a show of hands, which was most important to them, achievements or relationships. The vote was unanimous in favor of relationships. Then we asked which mattered most, outer appearances or who a person really was inside — his character, his true *nature. Everyone of course voted for the latter.*

Then we pointed out that the goals they had listed had more to do with achievements than with relationships, more to do with getting and doing than with being.

There were rebuttals that day. People said, "Well, setting goals is better suited to achievements than to relationships," and "What you do and what you have is what makes you who you are." But everyone (including us) left that day thinking about how we could focus more of our effort and more of our goals on the things we all know matter most.

It is possible to set goals that deal more with relationships and with character. It's possible, but it is difficult. A goal is "seeing" something the way you want it to be. When someone wants to make $100,000 a year, he sees himself in that circumstance and plots what he has to do to get there. When someone has a goal to lose weight, he sees himself thin and plans how to diet.

The same definition (and the same process) can apply to relationship and character goals, although it may be more *qualitative* and less quantitative. You can write a private *description* of a relationship as you want it to be, and that clear, written description can help you, even *cause* you to say and do things that bring it about. You can also write a description of the character and even the personality traits you want to have within yourself and let that mental picture become both a conscious and a subconscious guide for what you do and how you act.

So what is the new maxim that will remind us to judge and compete less, to think and work on relationships at least as much as achievements and on substance at least as hard as appearances?

Several useful and familiar sayings work in that direction. "Live and let live," "Win win," "Substance over style."

But in this case the best maxim is the oldest — the scriptural maxim that in slightly varying forms is a part of virtually every religion and enduring philosophy: "As a man thinketh in his heart, so is he."

For our new maxim let's adopt that ancient wisdom and add to it the naturally linked priority on relationships:

YOU ARE WHAT YOU THINK AND WHOM YOU LOVE.

We are not what we wear, or drive, or do, or eat. We are what we think. It is our most inner part — our thoughts — that we have the most opportunity to alter, and that is the part that will make the most difference.

LIVE FOR TODAY.

IF IT FEELS GOOD, DO IT.

It was a business associate who used to tell me that this was his motto. And in the context that he meant it, it had a certain appeal and validity. He was committed to living only in the present, to enjoying the moment.

The problem was he took it a step farther to where it meant, "Don't be bound by any convention or standard or even by any consequence." His goal was pleasure, which, by definition, made him selfish.

Too often in our society we are attracted to things that sound new rather than old, individualistic rather than conforming, and experimental and exciting rather than traditional and time-tested.

The problem is that many of us keep rediscovering an age-old wheel of folly. We end up learning, by trial and error (and by pain) things that millions of others have learned the same way and that philosophers, sages, prophets, and *God* have told us all along.

There was an interesting incident in our lay church where the congregation's leader (we call him a bishop) was a laborer by profession. He was sincere and dedicated but was neither educated nor articulate. One of the members in the same church was a highly trained (and very expensive) psychiatrist-therapist.

It so happened that several people from the church were going to both the bishop and the therapist for advice and counseling. Some of them felt that they were getting more help from the bishop, and they told the psychiatrist so. He was a little professionally troubled by this, so he went to the bishop and asked him what his secret was. What methods or teachings or counseling or therapy did he use which were so effective in helping people to improve their mental and emotional health?

The bishop took the question very seriously and gave a typically blunt answer. "Well . . . I just ask them questions until I figure out which commandment they are breaking, and then I tell them to stop it."

The word *commandment* sounds so authoritative and restrictive that we sometimes pull away and have the instinct to rebel, to "do our own thing." Yet scriptural commandments, for those who believe, are best described as "loving counsel from a wise father" — profound advice from a Supreme Being who wants us to be happy and has outlined the best behavioral ways to be so.

The simple fact is that there *are* absolutes. There are universal values that qualify as such through the collective human experience if not by their divine origin or source. And living by these ageless standards does not threaten or diminish our freedom, it *expands* it. There are consequences for selfish, indulgent behavior, and the consequences are usually in the form of *limits* — limited health, limited relationships, limited options and potential — in short, limited freedom.

My business associate's philosophy of instant gratification, living only for the present and doing whatever felt good at the moment worked well on some very important things, such as enjoying a pretty day or a current conversation or on feeling grateful for an unexpected opportunity or a serendipitous circumstance. But it worked terribly on things from the very temporal (credit cards and financial management) to the more spiritual (character, empathy and conscience).

The problem with his motto is that it pitted the

enjoyment of the present *against* the wisdom of the past and the prudent planning of the future. It was a choice of the one at the expense of the other two.

A Sanskrit poet saw things very differently. He believed that the present should be well lived, but with both the past and the future fully in mind: "Yesterday is but a dream and tomorrow only a vision, but today, well lived, makes every yesterday a dream of joy and every tomorrow a vision of hope."

People who value the past, both for its memories and for the wisdom of its experience, tend to understand and appreciate the present more and to have a clearer idea of where they want their own future to go. And minds that spend some time focused on the future usually have a clear enough sense of where they are going that they can worry less about it and thus enjoy the present more.

The new maxim represents a paradigm that has always been important — but never more so than today.

LIVE IN THE PAST, THE PRESENT, AND THE FUTURE, AND DO THE *RIGHT* THING.

In the long run, this *is* what feels good.

The funny thing about some of our most familiar cliches is that they are so outdated and meaningless that new generations mix them up and unintentionally produce hilarious hybrids.

A young Boston chef is stirring a soup tureen, telling his employer, "Spare the rod, spoil the broth." A San Diego child who had been incautious with fire is hospitalized with burns, and her young mother tells her, "You've cooked your goose, now lie in it." A boy working in a Saint Louis zoo declares, "Monkey do, but you can't make him drink it!"

An article in *The New Republic* cites a study in which 76 percent agreed with the statement that "it is impossible to see the forest while the cat was away," and 86 percent accepted that "blood is thicker than the milk of human kindness."

The same article suggests that some of the misquoted adages may subconsciously reflect a more accurate grasp of emerging political, social, and economic realities. Perhaps "a penny saved is worth two in the bush"; maybe "an empty barrel will keep the doctor away," and who's to disagree if someone says, "There's more than one way for every dog to do as the Romans do."

The first fourteen chapters replaced some old cliches on the subjects of attitudes, paradigms, and personal management. The final twelve chapters provide new maxims having more to do with priorities, relationships, and families — about the things that are the most important to us and the power we have to make them more like we want them to be.

PART TWO

Old Cliches and New Maxims About Priorities, Relationships, and Families

ALL YOU CAN DO IS ALL YOU CAN DO.

This cliche is often used as an antidote to other cliches that seem unrealistic and create false hopes: "The sky's the limit," "You can do anything you set your mind to," and so on.

Indeed it is good to be realistic, and it can be depressing and harmful always to expect more of ourselves than we actually deliver. So we say, "All you can do is all you can do."

Yet the things that inspire us most are instances and situations when someone seems to go *beyond* their natural potential, rise *above* the expected level, *beat* the odds.

Most of us, at least in the small, personal, everyday sense, believe in miracles. Love, loyalty, or other emotions sometimes carry us beyond what we thought we could do or feel. And in times of super-natural need, most of us believe in the possibility of some form of super-natural help.

I have a special friend who, over the years, has taught me a great deal about the word synergism. *He is a management consultant and trainer, and I first heard him speak of synergism in the business context. He defined the word as a situation where the total is greater than the sum of its parts, where executives or employees, working well together and compensating for one another's weaknesses, are able to accomplish more together than the combination of what they could accomplish separately.*

Later he taught me that as good a word as it was in business, synergism had its most magical application in personal and family life, where marriage partners, supporting and complementing each other, rise to a higher realm; where children feel a security and an identity bigger than themselves; where family members, helping and encouraging each other, grow and develop far beyond what they could do by themselves. In that context, synergism is the step we can take toward allowing miracles into our lives.

These are at least three types of synergism that allow us to do more and become more than we otherwise could:

1. PHYSICAL-MENTAL SYNERGISM. The mind and the body can be renewed by each other. When our minds are active, stimulated by new ideas, pulled out of the rut of routine, we are physically renewed, we feel more energy, and we are more resistant to disease. And when we take care of our body — when we eat right and exercise — our mind is quicker, sharper.

2. HUSBAND-WIFE SYNERGISM. Those who are married have the opportunity to create a union in which both partners, buoyed and lifted by each other, go beyond what they could do on their own. Too often we do the opposite. We compete with each other instead of finding ways to complement each other, and we think equality means doing the same things as each other rather than analyzing our individual strengths and weaknesses and figuring out who will play which roles within the family and household.

3. DIVINE SYNERGISM. The most powerful form of synergism and the instance when we can go farthest beyond our own potential or capacity is when we draw down into us a higher power and a greater insight. People who learn to pray, to meditate, to center themselves and exercise faith discover how limited they are by themselves and how unlimited they are with God.

The deeper meaning of synergism is that by ourselves we are limited, but that we can *combine* ourselves in ways that expand these limits. Combinations within ourselves, within our marriages, and within our spiritual lives can carry us beyond where we thought we could be. The ultimate display of synergism is miracles.

People who acknowledge or admit "ceilings" too readily take the excitement and possibility out of their lives. People stop progressing in their careers as soon as they say, "This is as far as I can get." People start to decline physically as soon as they say, "I'm over the hill." And discouragement and boredom set in when we say, "Well, realistically I'm never going to be what I once thought I could."

When our thoughts are bounded by limits, we need the simple new maxim:

BELIEVE IN MIRACLES.

The key to rising above our "ceilings" is not some kind of pseudo-pep talk or artificial "positive mental attitude." It is working at creating synergism in our lives and in our relationships. It is believing in something beyond ourselves.

LIVE TO WORK.

The Harvard Business School taught this one to me — or at least the prevailing environment and attitudes there did. I loved my time there and owe a lot to what I learned. But the attitude of work as the central experience of life and as the end rather than the means to other ends can be dangerous and damaging.

We've spoken already about the danger of making our work too big a part of our identity. But not doing so is a particular challenge in a world where the first question of most new conversations is, "What do you do?"

Is a job something we have or something we are?

In earlier times there was a certain *negative* social status attached to work. The lower your station, the more you had to work. The higher your place, the less you worked, the more you were able to enjoy leisure, or art, or travel, or whatever was your fancy. It certainly is social progress that in our more egalitarian society most everyone works who can work, and the work we do is by and large far more pleasant and fulfilling.

The question is whether some parts of our society have gone too far in glorifying work. Have careers been made to seem so stylish by society that we willingly let jobs consume us — giving up to them our time, our leisure, our nonwork friends, our broader interest in the world, and even our families?

I know people, and you do too, who make almost unbelievable sacrifices for career . . . without a second thought. They not only put in incredible amounts of time and energy, at the expense of almost everything else, but they also pick up and move to an unknown (or sometimes known but unpleasant) place, leaving family, home, and a lifestyle they love (things you'd think they'd fight for) at the whim of a transfer.

My best friend in high school and college was a remark-able case study of someone who went in the opposite direc-tion. His name, like mine, was Richard, and he taught me more than anyone else ever has about the art and enjoyment of living. His early death was a deep wound to my soul and left a void never quite filled.

The words life *and* live *had a meaning of excitement and relish to Richard, almost like a premonition of the fact that his life would be short and therefore must be full. Living, to Richard, meant experimenting, experiencing, enjoying. It also meant noticing and appreciating.*

Money, to him, was something you needed a certain amount of to live. And work was something you did for just long enough to get that money.

He would say, "Let's go!" and what he usually meant was "I've got enough to go to Acapulco, or to Alaska, or maybe just to Las Vegas." He traveled through Europe and other places by working somewhere long enough to have the money to go to the next place. Long-term saving was a hard concept for him, because money was to be used to do something or go somewhere — to learn and to enjoy — and sometimes to give to whoever seemed to need it more than he did.

Richard got a little more "responsible" as he matured and married. He became a gifted landscape architect and city plan-ner and loved his work. Yet he never lost his perspective. Work was good if it allowed him to do what he wanted to do and if it left him the resources and time to do the other things he wanted and to care for what he valued. If work helped him go where he wanted and let him be who he was, work was good. If it pulled him in unnatural directions or tried to own him, he dropped it or threw it out and looked elsewhere.

Work was for Richard a tool. If it extended him, increased his reach, his knowledge and power, served him and allowed him to do what he felt right about doing, then he valued the tool and took joy in it. But if it tried to turn on him, if it threatened to be the master rather than the servant, he handed it to someone else.

The president and CEO of a major, multinational computer company gave a remarkable speech wherein he described success as "nose prints on the window." He explained that the best measure of real accomplishment was how anxious your children are to see you when you come home from work. The same sentiment was expressed by a religious leader who said, "No other success can compensate for failure in the home." Still another said, "The most important work you will ever do will be within the walls of your own home."

Work is an important part of life. And that is the very point. Life is not a part of work.

Traveling the rural roads of a western state one summer, I struck up a conversation with a young couple who had, just a year before, left central Los Angeles and moved to a small mountain town. I asked them why. Their story was so basic and their explanation so simple, yet it had enormous resonance.

"We just asked ourselves one day, 'Why are we here?' We didn't like the schools; our streets weren't safe; none of our extended family was there; all we could afford was a small rented apartment with no yard. The *only* reason we were there was a job. We decided it was absurd to let a job dictate our lifestyle and even our values.

"We decided to switch it around, to put our *life* first and let our jobs follow. We found a place where we wanted to live, a place that was right for our children and that would let us live the way we wanted. We make half as much now, but we are at least twice as happy."

It's no mystery what the new maxim will be here. Another simple turnaround:

WORK TO LIVE.

LIVE BY YOUR LIST.

To see if you've fallen subject to this numbing notion, just ask yourself a question: When was the last time you did something that wasn't on your list, then *wrote it on* so that you could cross it off? It seems like we get our jollies these days by crossing things off our lists. The danger of course is that the lists become our masters rather than our tools. The "have-to-dos" take over our lives and keep us from any "choose-to-dos."

Studies show that the first conscious thought most of us have when we wake up in the morning is *What do I have to do today?* We make our lists and we go about it all day like good soldiers (or good slaves).

Our lists seem to get longer and longer because our

world grows more complex. The time management salesmen of the world want us to use *bigger* planners — with a space for every five minutes instead of one for every hour.

Yet we somehow know that it is not more *quantity* we need in our lives, it is more quality. We want more joy and more choice in life, not just more activity or more checks on our list.

A few years ago while still heavily into the "list mentality" I found myself on a family vacation in a place where the phone wasn't working.. After a couple of days of frustration at "not being able to get anything done," I made a strong, conscious effort to quit thinking about business, or the office, or the market, or anything (since I couldn't do much about any of them) I decided instead to really enjoy my family and my vacation.

I still had a hard time with the list addiction. I didn't feel right until I'd put something on paper each morning. So I still made lists — but I found that the things I was writing were now "choose-to-dos" instead of "have-to-dos." I was listing things like "talk to Josh about his classes for next year," or "walk down the beach," or "play Monopoly with Talmadge and Noah."

I felt so relaxed by the time that vacation was over that I resolved to keep putting some family needs and self-needs on my daily lists.

But it didn't work. There were so many things to do, especially after being away for two weeks. I'd make my list each day, and it was so long that I'd put off any family or personal notions to some other day.

The problem with a "things to do" list is revealed by the first word — *things*. Check your own lists and you will notice that they are made up mostly of *things* — not many *relationships,* or *ideas,* or *beauties,* or *rests,* or time to *sit and think.* The *things* crowd out the people, the "have-to-dos" dominate and leave no room for "choose-to-dos."

Try something — *not* easy. Try *resisting* thinking about what you have to do until *after* you have thought for a few moments about the real priorities. Ask yourself what you could do that day for family, or for friends, or for self. Think about *needs* and opportunities first, not about tasks and obligations. Decide on one choose-to-do each day for family and one for yourself. They need not be big or time-consuming — just something you thought about and decided to do, not because you had to but because you wanted to. Then when you make your list it will *include* the choose-to-dos and will seem more like a light and useful tool than a dark and oppressive master.

What we need in life is not more quantity but more quality. The time is *ours* and so are the choices. The *first* thing to do each day is to choose to do something for yourself and for your family. And the new maxim is:

PUT CHOOSE-TO-DOS AHEAD OF HAVE-TO-DOS.

THE HOME SUPPORTS THE CAREER.

It's not an individual that says this one to us — it's *society*! It is common to think about our work as the mainstream of our lives, the home only as a feeding tributary. The job becomes the place where our minds and hearts are, the home just a place to rest up and refuel. The career becomes our main base, the home just an orbiting support system. If one spouse stays home, it is to support the other spouse's career.

We hear questions commonly that are turned around, backward, cart-before-the-horse, upside-down questions such as, "How can I possibly have a child without interrupting or upsetting my career?" Or, "How can our marriage work when we both have such intense jobs?" Or, "Is there a way to start a real home or family when work takes all my time and energy?"

It's well and good (and necessary) to seek ways to balance home and work, but isn't the order and phrasing of these common questions a little contrary to life's true priorities? Shouldn't we be asking, "How can I keep my career without upsetting or compromising my family?" And, "How can we manage both of our careers when our marriage and relationship needs some time and effort?" And, "How can I handle my work in a way that gives me the time and energy I need for my family?"

What are the priorities here? And what are the *givens*? Is work primary and family secondary? Is career the goal and center of life and family merely the support and supplement? Does family just exist as some kind of support system to make it more convenient to work twelve hours a day? Are we married to our careers and just loosely employed in our home?

The questions bear some thought, because if we leave them unanswered with priorities unresolved, the window of time when we *can* do much with home and family will quickly pass.

Early in my career as a management and political consultant I was trying to service extra clients to build our busi-

ness. For an extended period I had to be in Iowa one day a week, Pennsylvania on another day each week, and San Juan, Puerto Rico, on a third day each week. The time in between was mostly spent traveling and trying to get back into the office enough to open mail and "catch up."

We had three small children, and Linda was staying home full-time to take care of them and to support my career. When we found the right support combination of help and schools, she would get back to her own career as a musician and writer.

We were trying to be creative, shaping ways that we could have children without compromising our professional goals.

We had lots of goals, and virtually all of them were stated (we had written them down) in terms of promotions, positions, gross income, and net worth.

About the only non-work-related reading I did in those days (mostly on red-eye flights when I couldn't sleep and had already finished the Wall Street Journal) was the work of C. S. Lewis. I'd gotten hooked on Lewis in college when I read his space trilogy and The Screwtape Letters. And I still devoted some time every summer vacation to reading his The Lion, the Witch, and the Wardrobe and the other Chronicles of Narnia to the children. I thought I had a copy of everything he'd ever published.

One night on a late flight I stumbled onto a new C. S. Lewis quote, one I'd not seen before and one that was to set me thinking (and questioning myself) in a direction that would precipitate many changes.

Lewis said (straight to me it seemed), "The homemaker

has the ultimate career. All other careers . . . exist for one pur-
pose only — and that is to support this ultimate career."

Perhaps it was because I'd had a frustrating day and was wondering if anything I did professionally really made any difference or had any real importance, or perhaps it was just because I respected C. S. Lewis too much to ignore anything he said. Whatever it was, I began to realize on that night that I was missing out on the most real and most important parts of life. My kids were growing up without me helping — or even noticing. My marriage was too often ignored. At worst I was using something very precious to support something very fleeting and temporary. At best I was working to support something that I wasn't very involved with.

We sometimes hear people say that they can't have children or take time for children because "My career is at such a critical point" or "I'm just at a stage right now when my work needs all my time."

The fact is that career needs are almost always more flexible than family needs. There is only a short "season" of our lives when we can have children, only a brief season when we are young with them, only a small time before we "turn around and they're gone."

If we acknowledge that what we do outside the home is to support what is inside our homes, if we acknowledge the seasons of our lives and don't neglect or put off what can only happen now, and if we try to think of ourselves not as principally a part of our companies or our jobs but as a part of our families, then our work will have deeper purpose and our homes will have more commitments and more security.

All we need do to turn the misleading cliche into a useful maxim is turn it around:

CAREERS EXIST TO SUPPORT HOMES.

CHAPTER 19

SPARE THE ROD, SPOIL THE CHILD.

First of all this one was never valid and certainly never wise. Its Biblical basis is metaphorical.

Children may become spoiled through a lack of any discipline from their parents, but the corporal, physical punishment this cliche advocates was never necessary, and if it can keep a child from becoming spoiled, it can also keep him from feeling loved, from developing confidence and freedom, and from reaching his full ability and potential.

The implication of the cliche is that children are trained the way animals are sometimes trained — not to do certain things because pain will be inflicted on them if they do.

The main problem with most parental discipline, or with parenting in general, is that it is aimed at *training* children to behave in a particular way so that they will be less trouble to us and more impressive to others. Instead we need to learn that discipline should be a means of *teaching* children correct principles and of helping them to find and love their best selves.

In a large parenting seminar that we were conducting, we asked the audience to name some of the hardest aspects of raising children — the things that bothered them most, that they spent the most time being troubled by, that they would like their children to change if they had one wave of a magic wand.

Hands went up, and the predictable answers came out: "Clean up after themselves," "Stop fighting and end sibling rivalries," "Accept responsibility for their tasks," "Obey me."

We talked for a time about various techniques and methods for developing more obedience, better order, less fighting, and so on. All seemed to agree that these ideas could make their households less hectic and their children less bothersome.

Then we asked a very different question — not what bothered or troubled them most in parenting but what the *deepest* danger *was, the greatest mistake they could make with the most lasting and serious consequences.*

Two answers emerged: (a) a permanent or long-term loss of communication — a breakdown of trust so that feelings and needs were no longer shared; and (b) the breaking of a child's fragile ego — the loss of his self-esteem or the thwarting of its growth.

Suddenly, right there in the meeting as we talked together as parents, we realized we were on a new level. What mattered most was not what worked best or what minimized inconvenience most. What mattered most was love, how much we shared and cared for each other, how well we communicated with each other, and how much self-esteem and individual security our love could give to our children. We realized how easy it is, sometimes, in our efforts to make children less bothersome and better behaved, to damage their egos and destroy relationships.

If our quest for perfect order, obedience, manners, and no-problem kids creates a constant barrage of correction and criticism and fear-based discipline, we may win the battle and lose the war. We may have neat, quiet homes containing insecure ego-damaged children.

Should we worry at all then about spoiling our children? Yes! But children are never spoiled by too much praise. Many children may have strong *wills,* but they all have fragile *egos.* Critical, insulting words; impatient, harsh tones; and any kind of corporal punishment can dent and damage these egos and can dampen and dim trust and communication.

Children do need rules, limits, and correction — in fact much of a child's security rests in knowing that his parents care about him and that his life does have rules and limits. But communication and self-esteem should always be the highest priorities. Time must be taken to talk about rules, to let the child help make them, to explain that they spring from love, and that we have them because children are important. And we must work on our tone, our look, our words, our touch — to see that they all build esteem rather than destroy ego.

It's hard to remember and hard to prioritize communication and the esteem of children when they seem to get in the way of our own convenience or the way we'd like things to work. It's hard, but a new maxim may help:

LOSE THE ROD, FIND THE CHILD.

In other words forget about convenience, military-like neatness, and efficiency. Forget about trying to make your child fit some perfect system you have in mind. Focus on the child instead — on who he is, what he needs, what he does well, and what he needs help with. Build your system around him rather than trying to build him into your system.

CHILDREN ARE LIKE LUMPS OF CLAY, AND PARENTS ARE THE SCULPTORS.

I read this in a parenting book! And it was an impressionable time for me because I had just become a parent. The general message seemed to be that children are so impressionable and pliable, especially in their early years, that parents can mold or fashion them into whatever they choose.

This notion is *not* some bit of traditional wisdom that has grown outdated and doesn't work anymore. It was never accurate, never even remotely true. It must have been born either out of ignorance and inexperience or out of a gross lack of respect for the individuality of children.

Oh, it certainly is true that children are impressionable and adaptable. The attitudes and examples of parents do have deep impact. And there is no question about the enormous *capacity* of small children to learn, to assimilate, to adapt. They can learn to play the violin at two, to read at three, to do square roots at four.

But to say they are lumps of clay that can be molded according to adult whims is to ignore the most important and most beautiful fact that parents can understand about their children — namely that they are each marvelously unique *individuals* possessing a particular set of gifts, potentials, and attributes that is theirs alone and unlike that of any other!

The reason the clay-molding metaphor is so dangerous is that so many parents have the inclination to make their children into themselves — or into what they wish they had been.

When our first son was born, the first comment I remember making was something like, "Look at those hands! He'll be palming a basketball by the time he's ten!" A few weeks later I put a basketball in his crib because it seemed more appropriate and more practical than a doll or stuffed animal. He'll get comfortable with it, I thought. Little Josh didn't show much interest in the ball as the months passed, but I kept tossing it back into the crib anyway.

When Josh was three years old, we were living in England, and I began to grow concerned that the future NBA star was being culturally deprived — there weren't any basketball games to take him to! Everyone played soccer, which didn't fit my grand design at all.

One morning a little ad in the London Times *informed me that the Harlem Globetrotters were coming to Wembley Arena, across the city from where we lived. I called and got two good seats and spent the next week trying to psyche Josh up for the great experience he would have.*

I assumed he would love basketball because I assumed he was a junior version of me — a sort of new and improved model of his dad, who would enjoy sports as much as I did but of course be much better at them than I had ever been!

Josh was impressed with the huge Wembley Arena and the noise of the crowd. And when the game started, he was very attentive and quiet — almost absorbed, I thought. But sometime midway through the first half I noticed that he was not actually watching the game. He was looking above the court, and his eyes were focused somewhere up in the air.

"What are you looking at, son?"

"Those numbers, Dad — up on that big thing. The two numbers on each side keep going up by twos, and the number in the middle keeps going down by one!"

Josh liked the scoreboard!

I remember thinking, during the second half, maybe this boy is different from me. Maybe he'll have his own unique set of interests and abilities. Maybe it's a mistake to try to turn him into what I was or I wanted to be.

That was the day I quit thinking of Josh as a lump of clay.

Today as a teenager Josh's room is filled with computers and quantitative software. He gives me programming lessons. He sees a whole world of data and information and numbers that is nearly invisible to me. Best of all, we admire and appreciate each other because of our differences.

What we need to do as parents is to *watch* and *perceive* as closely as we can — and to find out as early as we can *who* and *what* each of our children really is. They come with their own particular and unique sets of attributes, interests, gifts, and potentials, and the sooner we find out what these are, the better we can help them maximize what they can become.

A new maxim can serve to remind us of how special and unique each child is — and of how important it is that we try to find the reality of what is there rather than make it over into some preconception of our own.

CHILDREN ARE LIKE SEEDLINGS, AND PARENTS ARE THE GARDENERS.

Tiny seedlings often look the same — little green shoots — but one is an oak tree, one an elm, one a walnut tree, one a currant bush. No amount of manipulation or grafting will transform one into another or change their inner nature. The sooner we see who and what they are, the sooner we can tailor our gardening and nurturing to help them become the best of what they actually can be.

Good gardeners know that every tree, every bush, every flower is different, and caring gardeners watch each plant and know its nature well enough to know when to water, when to fertilize, when to prune.

ABILITY IS THE KEY
TO SUCCESSFUL PARENTING.

If a cliche is something that society begins to accept as traditional wisdom, then this has certainly become one! *Parenting* wasn't even a word we used until a few years ago, but now it's treated as a science, or an art, or at least a set of sophisticated methods or techniques. If you need to prove this to yourself, go into a bookstore and find the child-care or parenting section. It will be easy to find because it is a *big* section. You'll find books on every conceivable aspect of child rearing, and virtually all of them carry a tone of expertise, of step-by-step how-to, of technical ability that is intimidating.

The more books you pick up and look through, the more inadequate you feel. How can an ordinary person, without a Ph.D. or years of psychiatric experience, possibly succeed at something so complex as parenting?

When our first child was born, I was a graduate student, so I took the scholastic approach to parenting. I went down to the used-book store and picked up every child-rearing book whose author I had heard of. I ended up with eleven of them. My idea was to use spring break to speed-read the books, discover the points on which experts agreed, and adopt their consensus as my personal parenting philosophy.

Imagine my surprise when I discovered that they didn't agree on anything! Just when one author had won me over to a method or approach, I'd read an equally compelling contradiction from someone else. This "science" of parenting, as it turned out, wasn't "exact" at all; there were as many different opinions as there were writers.

The one good thing about the numerous points of disagreement I found was that I gradually became less intimidated. If the experts couldn't agree with each other, then I was under no obligation to agree with any of them. Besides, I noticed a couple of other disturbing things as I read. One was that several of these experts were not actually parents themselves. They had learned all this from other people's kids.

Some were practicing psychologists or psychiatrists whose main experience was with sick or troubled kids. And the tone of many of the books was negative — as though parenting were essentially a defense. "If Johnny does this, you do this," or "If you have this problem, try this response."

I decided I wanted to take the offensive rather than the defensive, and that while I might find some good general advice here and there, it wouldn't all apply to my kids. I think the main thing I gained through the process was a healthy skepticism of parenting "techniques" and authorities. (I even chanced upon a definition of expert *that said that an "ex" was a has-been, and a "spurt" was a drip under pressure.)*

If methods, techniques, expertise, and *ability* are not the keys to parenting, what is? Perhaps the answer is as easy to come up with as it is difficult to apply. Think about it. What do kids need? They need to be listened to, to be understood, to be valued. They need parents who will take the time to show them, teach them, help them, nurture them. They need to be made our priority, even when it is inconvenient.

They need the long-term commitments of quantity time rather than the quick fixes of "quality time" (which, by the way, is another extremely overused and counterproductive cliche).

I'll always remember a particular family who lived near us in northern Virginia. It was a large family, and the father was a laborer who struggled constantly to provide his family with the necessities. The mother worked part-time, in addition to caring for several small children. Despite their struggles there was a remarkable feeling of respect and cooperation in their house, a feeling I greatly admired but never fully understood.

Several years later, as I finished a lecture at a university, a young student came up and asked if I remembered her. It turned out that she had been one of the young children in that family. I took the opportunity to ask her what secret her parents had discovered and why their home had been so special and each child had turned out so well. I was especially interested in her father. "What did he do? What were his techniques?"

She smiled. "Come on — you remember my dad. He didn't deal in techniques. I'll tell you what he did do, though. He was always there for us. He never quit trying. We could always tell that we were the most important thing to him. I remember once, I was five or six years old, when he came to my room to apologize for blaming me for something I didn't do. I held his face in my hands and said, "It's okay, Daddy. I can tell how hard you're trying."

This is the easiest of yesterday's cliches to turn into a maxim that works today. We just add five letters to the beginning:

AVAILABILITY IS THE KEY TO SUCCESSFUL PARENTING.

The more we are there for our children, the longer they'll be there for us. What they need isn't our expertise, it's our attention.

Ability is not the key, availability is!

I WANT TO HAVE IT ALL.

The unofficial motto of the feminist movement has become a good general description of the most pervasive attitude of our time. "Having it all" has also become a tiresome cliche, with implications of greed, stress, and unrealistic expectations of ourselves.

Think about it. "Having it all" ignores the trade-offs, choices, and priorities that have always been a part of life. The central problem with the attitude is that it focuses on *wants* rather than *needs*. We want things because other people have them. We want to *do* and to *be* what we perceive those we envy to be doing and being. We want to have it and do it and be it *now*. And all without much reference to what we *need* or even to what would be best for ourselves and for those around us.

The old and healthy notion of *delayed gratification* is not much in fashion these days. "Saving up" or "waiting for" or even "looking forward to" are endangered phrases, if not already extinct. We buy it before we can afford it, do it when we don't have time for it, go after it even at the expense of time and focus taken from those we love and from things we can *only* do now.

I tuned in quite by chance to a late-night interview with one of the leading feminists of the last decade. She was once again a "current item" because she had recently, in her forties, given birth to her first child.

The interviewer, in a cynical tone, was boring in, trying to stir controversy or uncover inconsistency. "I'm going to read you a quote," he said, "and I want you to see if you know who said it: 'Any woman with any brains and any guts deserves to do something more important than staying home with little kids.' Do you know who said that?"

The camera focused on the guest, who sat forward and answered in a tone that mixed assurance and defiance. "I said it. Thank God I woke up before it was too late."

Without waiting for more questions (the interviewer had lost his train of thought anyway), she went on to say that in her rush and passion to do everything and be everything, she had almost literally forgotten to do what she now believed was the most important thing of all.

She talked in warm, mellow tones about how much her child had changed her paradigm, how much joy she had received, and how little she needed some of the things she had wanted so badly.

Then she rekindled her look of defiance and said something very powerful: "Look, I still want to have it all — I've just realized that I don't have to have it all at the same time!"

There are seasons in life. There is a time, for most, to have and raise children. There may be a time for public service, times for travel, times for intense concentration on career, times for education. And despite all sorts of popular myths about the shortness, the scarcity, and the "slipperiness" of time, the fact is that most normally healthy people in the spring, the summer, or even the fall of their lives have a *lot* of time. Learning to spend that time on what matters rather than trading it for things, for wants, for some illusive notion of having it all, is the lesson and perhaps the objective of life.

The opening cliche is not so bad — if it is modified first by a definition of *all* that means "all that I need and can use to contribute" and if we recognize that there is a right time and season for things and that delayed gratification is usually more of a joy than a sacrifice.

So — with those caveats — our new maxim:

HAVE IT ALL — BUT NOT ALL AT THE SAME TIME.

FAMILIARITY BREEDS CONTEMPT.

What does this one mean anyway? I've heard it all my life to the point that its repetition gives it credibility. I asked one friend what he thought it meant, and he said, "There are two things you should never watch being made — hot dogs and laws." His point was that the *actuality* behind some things ruins any illusions we have of their purity. When we get to *know* things or people, we see their faults, their imperfections, and supposedly we begin to despise them or hold them in contempt.

But is it really so?

Or is the opposite closer to the truth? Isn't it nearly

impossible not to care for something or someone we really know? When we know someone, "warts and all," don't we inevitably develop an empathy, a concern, a caring? Isn't it a *lack* of interest, a *lack* of understanding, that breeds suspicion, enmity, and disdain?

The problem with this old cliche is that it gives a kind of *sanction* to the deterioration of a relationship. Marriages end in divorce because we "get to know each other too well." We move too often and fail to put down roots because we're "tired of the same old place." The grass is always greener on the other side of the fence (to use a closely related cliche), because we're unsatisfied with the familiar.

As a college student I worked one summer as an intern for a U. S. senator in Washington, D.C. In an effort to save money while driving back west to school in the fall, I advertised on the intern bulletin board for a passenger to share the trip with me. The night before I was to leave, I got a call from someone who introduced herself as Kathy and said she was headed for Colorado and would love a ride. I told her I was in a hurry and wanted to drive straight through, and she said she had no problem with that. She sounded pleasant and enthusiastic (even attractive, I imagined) so I agreed to pick her up the next morning.

The best way to explain what happened the next morning is bluntly. Kathy weighed three hundred pounds. She had nothing with her but a huge tattered foot locker (we were forced to tie the trunk lid partially closed to accommodate it) and a big paper bag full of bananas. She was not a Senate intern but had noticed my card on the bulletin board one day while she was roaming around "trying to get a glimpse of Teddy Kennedy." And she was not returning to school, she just wanted to see Colorado because she had "heard it was pretty."

It gets worse. She ate bananas nonstop, tossing the yellow peels nonchalantly over her shoulder into the back seat. She had an opinion on everything, always negative, including my car, my driving, the broken air-conditioning, and the humid weather. After five or six hours I said I was getting a little sleepy and asked her if she'd take a turn at the wheel. "Oh, I don't drive," she said. I was flabbergasted. "How will we drive straight through?" I asked. "I'm really good at keeping people awake," she answered.

The third time we stopped for gas, I asked her if she might want to pay this time. I almost expected the answer I got, "Oh, I don't have any money!"

I'll spare you the rest of the details. The point is that the trip took forty-two hours and that unfamiliarity bred contempt that was gradually dissolved by familiarity. Since there was nothing to do but talk (and it did keep me awake), we gradually got acquainted. Her bizarre habits and appearance were easier to understand as I came to know her past

147

— orphaned, raised in poverty by an elderly grandmother, trying now to find a place where she could escape her past and start fresh. There was an interesting, refreshing candor about her, no pretense, no ax to grind. After I got past judging her and resenting the situation — and started listening because there was nothing better to do — I found myself liking her.

As with so many of these old cliches, the problem is that accepting it causes negative or counterproductive behavior. If we believe that familiarity breeds contempt, it can cause us to "keep our distance," to hold ourselves back from really knowing others or fully revealing ourselves.

What we need in the world, and what most of us need in our individual lives, is not more facades or more isolation but more openness, more candor, more of being ourselves and sharing ourselves, more of saying and less of leaving things unsaid (see next chapter).

Commitment is a word that seems to go in and out of fashion. Avoiding it, we sometimes tell ourselves, gives us freedom and autonomy. But in fact the only guarantees of no commitments are loneliness and purposelessness.

It is commitment that gives us strength and vision, and commitment makes us unafraid of familiarity.

The reason nearly half of today's marriages end in divorce is that we have let ourselves become wary of a good marriage's two necessities: commitment and familiarity. In the security of a total commitment, a complete sharing and total familiarity can develop that breeds empathy, understanding, and love.

The new maxim:

COMMITMENT IS WHAT ALLOWS FAMILIARITY WITHOUT CONTEMPT.

SOME THINGS ARE BETTER LEFT UNSAID.

My grandmother again! And again, she was right in some circumstances and in some relationships. There certainly are times to hold our tongues, to agree to disagree, to avoid criticism and conflict. Even Thumper knew that (one of Grandmother's favorites) and shared his knowledge with Bambi: "If you can't say sumthin' nice, don't say anythin' at all."

So what's the problem?

The problem is *communication*. Way too much goes unsaid these days. Way too many feelings get bottled up. Way too many marriages and other important relationships turn stale or ugly or simply *end* because too much is left unsaid.

Consider, as an extreme example, the story of Alf and Anna from the old country. Anna said, "Alf, we're married twenty-five years now and you never tell me you love me." Answers Alf, "Anna, I told you I loved you the day we were married. If anything changes, I'll let you know!"

It's not only the positive things that we need to say, it's the concerns, the frustrations, the hurts, and the feelings that need to get out, get aired, get communicated, get understood.

My wife, Linda, grew up with two marvelous parents who resembled Alf and Anna. Actually they both resembled Alf. Her father was a quiet, stoic man who worked hard and had deep loyalties but who showed his affections more through a twinkle in his eye than through anything he ever said. Her mother is a delightful, energetic woman who, in her eighties, still goes bowling twice a week and occasionally plays volleyball, but still keeps most feelings to herself.

Linda remembers from her childhood that when her mother felt a little anger or frustration with her father, she had the habit of going into the kitchen and slamming the knife-and-

fork drawer a couple of times. The metallic crashing sound was both therapeutic and slightly symbolic of how her insides felt.

I observed some of these "silent techniques" in Linda's parents while we were dating, and we committed ourselves to more openness and to the sharing of feelings. We would always say it, good or bad, positive or negative, so long as it was honest. All of this committing makes one certain day about two weeks after our wedding particularly memorable (and illustrative of how hard it is to change things that we've grown up with).

Sitting in the tiny living room/bedroom of our student housing apartment, I did something that made Linda very angry and upset. Her face turned red and her eyes looked daggers in my direction, but she said nothing. Instead she got up, strode into the kitchen, and slammed the knife-and-fork drawer as hard as she could.

Hopefully in each of our marriages and families the goal is unity — even "oneness." Yet there can't be true oneness when there are hidden feelings or secrets. The question in this context is not whether we should express our feelings — we *should*. The question is *how* and *when*.

"When" is not always at the moment you feel the most upset, and "how" is not always with the first words that come to mind, but expressing feelings — getting them out — is a must within a marriage.

There is something remarkably powerful and surprisingly *secure* about a relationship in which everything is shared and nothing is hidden. Such a relationship requires real commitment and love, and it unfolds and opens with the goal of becoming *one,* even as you hold on to individuality. When this happens, our lives begin to feel a completion that is impossible in any other way.

The new maxim sounds a little ghoulish — a little like Halloween — but most married couples who think about it know that it is true:

—

UNEXPRESSED FEELINGS NEVER DIE, THEY JUST GET BURIED AND COME FORTH LATER IN UGLIER FORMS.

—

LOVE MEANS YOU NEVER HAVE TO SAY YOU'RE SORRY.

This cliche came from (or at least was popularized) by the movie *Love Story*. Then it was made into a song and really worked itself into our consciousness.

What does it mean anyway? It seems to me that the more in love you are and the more intense your love and emotions are, the *more* you may need to say you're sorry. And what's so bad about saying you're sorry? I like the other lovers' cliche that says, "The best part of fighting is that it's so much fun to make up."

The ideal marriage is not some antiseptic alliance in which people understand and empathize so perfectly and become so identical to each other that they never disagree, never get angry, never have to apologize. A conflict-free, apology-free marriage, if you'll forgive a comparison almost as trite as some of the cliches, would be as boring (and eventually as dead) as endless, perfect sunny weather with never a wind or a raindrop or a storm.

There was a marvelous ninety-two-year-old gentleman who used to go to church where we do. One Sunday, in a classroom setting, someone asked him how he had lived so long — the secret of his longevity. He thought for a moment and then started telling us an incident from early in his marriage. Because he was hard of hearing, we thought he had missed the question. But he went on:

"Way back seventy years ago when my wife and I got married," he said, "we pledged to each other that we would never fight or argue within the walls of our home." He paused with a twinkle in his eye before continuing. "That's why we've lived so long — we've spent so much time in the out of doors."

Not long after that I happened to sit next to a marriage counselor on a plane. He'd been in practice for more than thirty years. I asked him if he'd run into any conflict-free marriages. "Sure," he said, "lots of them. They all fit into one of three categories: marriages where one spouse is dead; marriages where one spouse is completely dominant and the other is a total doormat; and marriages of convenience where the two parties have so little to do with each other that they never conflict."

The marital challenge lies not in forever ending conflict but in learning to resolve differences in ways that build and benefit rather than hurt and harm.

And it's not the end of the world if your children see you disagree — so long as you also let them see you resolve and work things out. Kids who grow up without ever seeing a conflict between their parents will have unrealistic expectations of their own marriages.

Interestingly, the four things we most *need* to communicate *about* as marriage partners are also the four areas where conflict or argument most often occurs: child rearing, money, sex, and goals or aspirations. In all four areas communication, even with a lot of bumpy disagreement and resolution, is far better than noncommunication.

There are two very basic "communication adjustments" that are particularly useful in disagreements in any of the four areas. (1) Start sentences with "I feel" instead of with "You are." It's harder to hurt and easier to understand when you start with "I feel." (2) Paraphrase and repeat what the other person said before making your point. When we argue we're too often just thinking of what we're going to say next — and we don't listen. If you have to repeat the other person's point before you make your next point, you'll listen and understand more and short-circuit many arguments.

At least as important as how we say the negative things is that we don't forget to say the positive things. A good way to do both is to have a short "partnership meeting" once a week. Try a "feelings expression" where each of you takes a few minutes to tell each other how you *feel* . . . about each other, about the children, about the past week. In that few minutes the negative feelings or times you've felt hurt or offended can also come out — in a way that has a good chance of being understood and of not being bitter or hurtful.

This weekly "clearing of the air" is more practical than a couple of other old cliches: "Never let the sun set on a disagreement," or "Never go to bed angry," both of which can keep people up all night.

So again the new maxim is a reversal of the old cliche:

LOVE MEANS SAYING "I'M SORRY" AS OFTEN AS NECESSARY AND "I LOVE YOU" AS OFTEN AS POSSIBLE.

HE WHO DIES WITH THE MOST TOYS WINS.

A popular bumper sticker? Or a penetrating, one-sentence summary of current Western society?

"More is better."

"Bigger is better."

"Money is how we keep score."

The problem is that "*more*" becomes an end in itself rather than the means to some other end. We are obsessesed with *more*, and it's not a new phenomenon.

Bertrand Russell warned us that "it is the preoccupation with possessions, more than any other thing, that keeps man from living freely and nobly."

And maybe e. e. cummings said it even better: "More, more, more, more. My hell, what are we all, morticians?"

It's easy to blame our "morishness" on our society and its institutions. A friend of mine, who is a senior vice president of one of New York's largest ad agencies, is remarkably candid in defining his own profession. "Advertising," he said, "is the finely honed art of getting people to think they need what they really only want."

Everyone should have a favorite bookstore. To go in and browse once in a while is not only pleasant, it is a quick update on trends, fads, and directions.

Lately I see a lot on simplifying and getting back to basics. These are always popular subjects, but they do better at certain times than at others.

I have a favorite bookseller in my favorite bookstore, and he told me the other day that Thoreau is selling again. "You can chart society by Thoreau," he said. "When he starts to sell, you know we're getting tired of materialism and the fast lane. The last time Thoreau sold was in the sixties."

I realized as he said it that the last time I had read Thoreau was in the sixties. I carried Walden around with me for two years. I even drove out to Walden Pond several times while I was a student in Boston, wanting to feel as much of the writer's wisdom as I possibly could.

My friend the bookseller said, "Here's a new edition of his collected works," and scurried off to help another customer. I let it fall open, and Thoreau was talking about how the land he surveyed was more "his" than it was the man who owned it — because he saw and appreciated and took pleasure from the land.

I thumbed the book at random to another spot and read, "Our life is frittered away by detail, simplify! Simplify! Simplify!

I let it fall open again, and Thoreau was comparing owning a farm to being in jail — the encumbering, enslaving aspects of ownership.

The lunch hour was over, but as I put the book down, I wondered if I should go back to work.

The world, and particularly Western society, is afflicted with an erroneous notion called "ownership."

Our perceptions of ownership are wrong in two ways. First they are wrong because they are inaccurate. What we say we own actually just passes through our hands for a time. It really belongs to nature or to God, depending on your perception. We have our "possessions" just for a period, so *stewardship* is actually a more accurate term than *ownership.*

The second way an ownership mentality is wrong is that it is morally wrong — or at least it leads to thoughts and to acts that often are. In the ownership mode everyone has more or less of something than we do, so there is envy, jealousy, or covetousness on the one hand or pride and condescension on the other.

And when we begin to think we own our children, or our talents, or even our bodies, rather than perceiving them as gifts from God, we tend to value them less and to use them ever more selfishly.

Stewardship is a wonderful concept. It implies caring and responsibility without pride or envy. The best parents I know think of themselves as stewards over incredibly precious and ultimately independent children. The happiest people I know are the ones who are really grateful for what they have but are not attached to things or preoccupied with having more.

The cliche that opened the chapter is often meant to be funny. But its practice seldom is. In actuality he who dies with the most toys (or the most money) probably stands the best chance of his children or descendants fighting over them.

A steward doesn't necessarily want more. He wants to do his best with what he has. He wants more quality in his life rather than more quantity.

THINK STEWARDSHIP, NOT OWNERSHIP.

CLICHE
MAXIM

Here's a look at the complete list. Twenty-six old cliches that we ought to toss out and twenty-six new maxims to help our attitudes and approaches fit better with both the realities and the opportunities of today.

To have much effect, each new maxim needs to be *worked on* a bit. It needs to be worked into the subconscious so that it begins to influence how we think and act. It's hard to do this with all twenty-six at once. A suggestion: Read through the list and pick the old cliches that you think you are *subject* to, then work on the new maxims that replace them.

To help you do that, let's summarize with a parallel list of the twenty-six old and the twenty-six new.

PART ONE

Old Cliches and New Maxims About Attitudes, Paradigms, and Personal Management.

CHAPTER	THE OLD CLICHE	THE NEW MAXIM
1	If a thing is worth doing, it's worth doing well.	If a thing is just barely worth doing, then just barely do it.
2	Never put off until tomorrow what you can do today.	Always put off a "put-offable" in favor of a now or never.
3	Work before play.	Stale work is renewed by fresh play.
4	Don't just sit there, do something!	Don't just do something, sit there.
5	Get serious!	The reason angels can fly is that they have learned to take themselves lightly.
6	Act, don't re-act.	Act and respond.
7	Hurry up.	Seek the speed of going slow.

CHAPTER	THE OLD CLICHE	THE NEW MAXIM
8	Plan your work and work your plan.	Be firm on the goal, but flexible on the plan.
9	A change is as good as a rest.	Nothing is as good (or as necessary) as real rest.
10	You made your bed, now lie in it.	Get out of your bed before it gets too comfortable.
11	Keep your nose to the grindstone.	Enjoy the journey.
12	There's a time and place for everything.	Know when *this* is the place and *now* is the time.
13	You are what you eat (or wear, or drive, or live in, or do).	You are what you *think* and whom you love.
14	Live for today. If it feels good, do it.	Live in the past, the present, and the future, and do the *right* thing.

PART TWO

Old Cliches and New Maxims About Priorities, Relationships, and Families.

CHAPTER	THE OLD CLICHE	THE NEW MAXIM
15	All you can do is all you can do.	Believe in miracles.
16	Live to work.	Work to live.
17	Live by your list.	Put choose-to-dos ahead of have-to-dos.
18	The home supports the career.	Careers exist to support homes.
19	Spare the rod, spoil the child.	Lose the rod, find the child.
20	Children are like lumps of clay, and parents are the sculptors.	Children are like seedlings and parents are the gardeners.

CHAPTER	THE OLD CLICHE	THE NEW MAXIM
21	Ability is the key to successful parenting.	*Availability* is the key to successful parenting.
22	I want to have it all.	Have it all — but not all at the same time.
23	Familiarity breeds contempt.	Commitment is what allows familiarity without contempt.
24	Some things are better left unsaid.	Unexpressed feelings never die, they just get buried and come forth later in uglier forms.
25	Love means you never have to you're sorry.	Love means saying "I'm sorry" as often as necessary and "I love you" as often as possible.
26	He who dies with the most toys wins.	Think stewardship, not ownership.

As I look back over these twenty-six new maxims, it occurs to me that they all relate in some way to *prioritizing* and *balance*. They also seem to embody the following four principles:

- Honor relationships over achievements
- Select quality over quantity
- Value "choose-to-dos" over "have-to-dos"
- Believe in spontaneity as much as structure

It's not that achievements, quantity, have-to-dos, and structure are unimportant. It's just that they get too much attention in our competitive, list-oriented, materialistic world. Each of the new maxims, in its own way, says something about balancing life by moving quality, spontaneity, relationships, and choose-to-dos up into parity and perhaps ahead of their counterparts.

May we internalize these principles. May we exercise and implement the new maxims. May we enjoy life more and live it more fully.

— Richard Eyre

F O L L O W   U P
Joining HOMEBASE and getting "Lifebalance"

Believe it or not, there is a whole group of busy, overcommitted people who are already very involved in seeking the more balanced, more quality-oriented lifestyle suggested by the twenty-six new maxims.

The worldwide co-op S.J.S. HOMEBASE includes over fifty thousand parents who receive monthly materials on family and quality-oriented lifestyles and "Lifebalance" and who often form small neighborhood groups with other HOMEBASE members to assist one another with family objectives and the cultivation of more productive, less stressful attitudes.

To receive a free HOMEBASE membership catalog and explanatory audiotape, please call (801) 581-0112 or send in the card on the facing page.

By the way, when you call or write, tell us about any other old cliches that bother you or seem outdated or inconsistent with how we live and what we need today. Help us out with the second volume of maxims.

CARD

To obtain a free catalog of HOMEBASE parenting and family programs, and an overview audio tape by Linda and Richard Eyre, send the card below, along with $5.00 for postage and handling, to:

HOMEBASE
1615 South Foothill Drive
Salt Lake City, UT 84108   Or call (801) 581-0112.

. . . is an international co-op of parents dedicated to making children and family their first priority and to the fostering of traditional values and correct principles in all of our institutions and in society at large.

For preschoolers "TCJ" (Teaching Children Joy) or "Joy Schools" - In-home, do-it-yourself neighborhood preschools focusing on the physical, mental and social "joys" of childhood.

For elementary age children "TCR" (Teaching Children Responsibility) - A program (stories, discussions, music) to conduct around the dinner table that teaches all forms of responsibility and self reliance.

For all ages but particularly adolescents "TCV" (Teaching Children Values) - A once-a-week Sunday program — materials and audio tapes to teach sensitivity, honesty and other values.

For busy parents "LFB" (Lifebalance) - A video and audio tape seminar with fill-in-the blank materials on how to balance family, work and personal needs.

Yes! I am interested in the possibility of membership in HOMEBASE. Please send me further information about:

☐ TCJ   ☐ TCV
☐ TCR   ☐ LFB

Name _____ Phone _____
                                              area code / number
Address _____
              street
_____
              city / state / zip

Richard Eyre's life illustrates a movement from cliches to maxims.

A Harvard MBA, he founded three companies, held two White House appointments, ran for governor, believed most of the cliches, and thought maybe he could change the world a bit through achievements in the public and private sectors.

Today he spends more time with his children, hosts a national TV show called *Families Are Forever* with his wife Linda, believes the maxims, works to promote volunteerism, and thinks maybe the world and its values can be saved . . . one family at a time.